Verilog® HDL Synthesis
A Practical Primer

Other books by the same author:

- *A Verilog HDL Primer,* Star Galaxy Press, Allentown, PA, 1997, ISBN 0-9656277-4-8.
- *A VHDL Synthesis Primer, Second Edition,* Star Galaxy Publishing, Allentown, PA, 1998, ISBN 0-9650391-9-6. (Based on IEEE Std 1076.3-1997 Arithmetic Packages, NUMERIC_BIT and NUMERIC_STD)
- *A VHDL Synthesis Primer,* Star Galaxy Publishing, Allentown, PA, 1996, ISBN 0-9650391-0-2.
- *A VHDL Primer: Revised Edition,* Prentice Hall, Englewood Cliffs, NJ, 1995, ISBN 0-13-181447-8. (Based on IEEE Std 1076-1993)
- *A VHDL Primer,* Prentice Hall, Englewood Cliffs, NJ, 1992, ISBN 0-13-952987-X. (Based on IEEE Std 1076-1987)
- *A Guide to VHDL Syntax,* Prentice Hall, Englewood Cliffs, NJ, 1995, ISBN 0-13-324351-6.
- *VHDL Features and Applications: Study Guide,* IEEE, 1995, Order No. HL5712.
- **In Japanese**: *A VHDL Primer,* CQ Publishing, Japan, ISBN 4-7898-3286-4, 1995.
- **In German**: *Die VHDL-Syntax* (Translation of *A Guide to VHDL Syntax*), Prentice Hall Verlag GmbH, 1996, ISBN 3-8272-9528-9.

Verilog® HDL Synthesis
A Practical Primer

J. BHASKER

Distinguished Member of Technical Staff
Bell Labs, Lucent Technologies

Star Galaxy Publishing
1058 Treeline Drive, Allentown, PA 18103

Published by:

Star Galaxy Publishing
1058 Treeline Drive, Allentown, PA 18103
Phone: 610-391-7296

Cover design: Jennifer Swanker

WARNING - DISCLAIMER
The author and publisher have used their best efforts in preparing this book and the examples contained in it. They make no representation, however, that the examples are error-free or are suitable for every application to which a reader may attempt to apply them. The author and the publisher make no warranty of any kind, expressed or implied, with regard to these examples, documentation or theory contained in this book, all of which is provided "as is". The author and the publisher shall not be liable for any direct or indirect damages arising from any use, direct or indirect, of the examples provided in this book.

Printed in the United States of America

10 9 8 7 6 5

Library of Congress Catalog Card Number: 98-61058

ISBN 0-9650391-5-3

Zindagi ka safar, hai ye kaisa safar,
("Life's travel, what a travel it is")
Koi samjha nahi, koi jana nahi,
("No one has understood it, no one knows about it")
Hai ye kaisi dager, chalte hai sub mager,
("What kind of goal it is, still everyone goes through it")
Koi samjha nahi, koi jana nahi
("No one has understood it, no one knows about it")

- A song from an Indian film "Safar"

CONTENTS

❑

FOREWORD

The topic of Verilog HDL synthesis has been in existence since 1988. However good textbooks on the topic have not covered basic concepts until now. This practical primer on Verilog HDL synthesis provides a comprehensive and practical description for this new technology. It takes the mystery out of HDL synthesis, by providing an easy to understand Verilog language semantic with respect to synthesis technology. Bhasker is an expert on synthesis: he has worked in synthesis for more than fourteen years. He is currently using his expertise in leading the efforts as the chair of IEEE working group for developing a Verilog RTL synthesis standard (PAR 1364.1) that is based on the OVI[1] RTL synthesis subset 1.0 released in April 1998. Bhasker is one of the architects for the OVI standard on RTL synthesis.

"Verilog HDL Synthesis, A Practical Primer" by J. Bhasker provides students and practicing logic designers with immediate access to well-organized information about Verilog HDL synthesis. It is easy to read and provides a very large number of examples of synthesizable Verilog HDL models. The reader is led systematically from Verilog HDL language constructs, their meaning in synthesis, how synthesis design technology transforms such constructs into gates, and their impact on design verifica-

1. Open Verilog International

tion. The book is rich in Verilog HDL model examples and their gate equivalence. The examples are simple and show the different styles of logic modeling such as combinational logic, sequential logic, and register and latched based design, finite state machines, arithmetic units and others.

The book is not just unique in covering HDL synthesis for beginners, but also goes into advanced topics such as how to get optimized logic from a synthesis model. Resource sharing and allocation is one of the topics covered under model optimization. Another unique topic is design verification. The book goes into the principles of synthesis model writing to ensure predictable and verifiable results. Although the chapter is intended for simulation, the same concepts can be applied for formal verification.

This book is the first comprehensive treatment for Verilog HDL synthesis. Bhasker has taught Verilog HDL and Verilog HDL synthesis at Lucent Technologies for more than three years. The book shows the knowledge that Bhasker has accumulated during his fourteen years on synthesis. Although this book is targeted for beginners, expert users can benefit from the basic principles as well as the advanced modeling topics in synthesis. Definitely, intellectual property (IP) developers should follow the modeling style recommended in this book.

Vassilios C. Gerousis
Senior Staff Technologist, Motorola, Phoenix, Arizona
Chairman, Technical Coordinating Committee (TCC), Open Verilog International

PREFACE

Here is a practical and useful guide to Verilog HDL register-transfer level synthesis. A large number of synthesizable Verilog HDL examples are provided. Verilog HDL constructs that are supported for synthesis are described in detail. Furthermore, examples are shown using these synthesizable constructs collectively to model hardware elements. Common causes of functional mismatches between the design model and the synthesized netlist are described in detail and recommendations are made on how to avoid these.

To many, synthesis appears like a black-box; a design described in Verilog HDL goes in, and out comes a gate level netlist. It appears as if there is some mystique in this black-box approach. To take full advantage and usefulness of a synthesis system, it is important to understand the transformations that occur during the synthesis process. The purpose of this book is to expose the black-box myth by describing the transformations that occur during the synthesis process from a hardware description language model to a netlist; Verilog HDL is used as the modeling language.

The Verilog Hardware Description Language, often referred to as Verilog HDL, is an IEEE standard (IEEE Std 1364). The language can be used to describe the behavior, sequential and concurrent, or structure of a model. It can support the description of a design at multiple levels of abstraction ranging from the architecture level to the switch level. The language provides support for modeling a design hierarchically and in addition, provides a rich set of built-in primitives, including logic gates and user-defined primitives. Precise simulation semantics are associated with all the language constructs and therefore models written in this language can be verified using a Verilog HDL simulator.

Synthesis, in general, has a different meaning to different people. In this book, I refer to synthesis of a design described in Verilog HDL; this design describes combinational logic and/or sequential logic. In case of sequential logic, the clocked behavior of the design is expressly described. This precludes talking about logic synthesis (a design described in terms of primitive gates) and about high-level synthesis (behavior specified with no clocking information). The synthesis process transforms this Verilog HDL model into a gate level netlist. The target netlist is assumed to be a technology-independent representation of the modeled logic. The target technology contains technology-independent generic blocks such as logic gates, and register-transfer level (RTL) blocks such as arithmetic-logic-units and comparators. The succeeding phases of a synthesis process, which are technology translation (that is, mapping of generic gates to specific parts in a library) and module binding (that is, building RTL blocks using primitive gates) are not described in this book.

It is difficult to write a book on synthesis due to its rapidly evolving nature. In this book, I have therefore provided the basic information that will hold true by and large. I have tried to stay clear of ambiguous topics including implementation-specific issues. Because of the richness of the Verilog HDL language, there may be more than one way to describe a certain behavior. This book suggests one or two such modeling styles that are synthesizable. Again, not all constructs in the language can be synthesized since Verilog HDL was designed to be a simulation language. Therefore, in this book, I have showed constructs that would be supported by a majority of synthesis systems.

I have also avoided mentioning the various features of vendor-specific synthesis tools. However, there are certain cases when it becomes necessary to show an example of an implementation. In such a case, the feature is shown as it is implemented in the ArchSyn (version 14.0) synthesis system developed at Bell Labs, Lucent Technologies.

CAUTION: Not all available synthesis systems may support the Verilog HDL constructs described in this book. For more details on spe-

cific features of any synthesis system, the reader is urged to consult the respective vendors' documentation.

A Verilog Synthesis Interoperability Working Group, of which I am the Chair, is at present working to develop an IEEE standard for RTL synthesis.

This book assumes that the reader knows the basics about the Verilog HDL language. A good source to get such information is the precursor of this book "*A Verilog HDL Primer*", published by Star Galaxy Press.

This book is targeted to electrical engineers, specifically circuit and system designers, who are interested in understanding the art of synthesis. The book does not try to explain any of the synthesis algorithms. My belief is that by understanding what results to expect from synthesis, a designer will be able to control the quality of the synthesized designs by writing effective design models. This is because the synthesized structure is very sensitive to the way in which a certain model is written.

This book can be used as a text in a college course. In an electrical engineering curriculum, this book can be used in a VLSI course on computer-aided design. Students may use this book to write models and synthesize these using any available synthesis system. The transformations occurring during the synthesis process can thus be studied. In a computer science course, such as in an algorithms course on computer-aided design, students may write a simple synthesis program that reads in a subset of Verilog HDL and generates a synthesized netlist. Examples in this book can be used as test cases to understand the generated netlist.

Professional engineers will greatly benefit from this book when used as a reference. The presence of many examples with models and their synthesized netlists help an engineer in directly going to the page of interest and exploring the example models presented there.

Book Organization

Chapter 1 describes the basics of the synthesis process. The basics include topics such as what is a wire, a flip-flop or a state, and how the sizes of objects are determined.

Chapter 2 describes the mapping of Verilog HDL constructs to logic gates. It gives examples of combinational logic and shows how the Verilog HDL constructs get transformed into basic gates and interconnections. Styles for modeling sequential logic designs are also described along with examples for modeling asynchronous preset and clear, synchronous preset and clear, multiple clocks, and multiple-phase clocks.

Occasionally it becomes necessary to use pre-designed blocks in a design. Chapter 2 further describes how to model structure, including the capability to model partial structure in a behavior model.

Chapter 3 describes how Verilog HDL constructs are collectively used to model hardware elements. While Chapter 2 describes the mapping of Verilog HDL to logic gates, this chapter describes the opposite scenario, which is, how to model a hardware element in Verilog HDL for synthesis. Elaborate examples are provided for many common hardware elements, such as multiplexers, counters, decoders and arithmetic-logic-units.

Chapter 4 describes powerful techniques that can be applied to a Verilog HDL model to provide quality synthesized netlists. The optimizations described in this chapter may be performed automatically by a synthesis system; if not, it may have to be performed manually by the designer to achieve quality results.

Having synthesized a Verilog HDL model, it is often necessary to validate the synthesized netlist with the input design model. Chapter 5 provides testbench writing strategies that can be used to verify the synthesis results. Because Verilog HDL is not specifically designed to be used as a synthesis language, functional differences may occur between the design model and the synthesized netlist. This chapter explains the cause of some such discrepancies.

In order to illustrate a subset of Verilog HDL supported for synthesis by a typical synthesis system, Appendix A provides a construct by construct description of what is supported by the ArchSyn synthesis system. However, such a subset may vary between different synthesis systems.

Appendix B presents the description of logic gates that are used in the synthesized netlists described in this book.

The synthesized netlists shown in this book are NOT optimized netlists; thus the logic shown in some cases may be suboptimal. This is acceptable since the purpose of this book is to show the transformation of Verilog HDL to gates and not that of demonstrating logic optimization techniques. Some of the netlists have been optimized purposely so that the netlist could be captured as a figure in the book.

Conventions

The term designer is referred to in many places in the text. It is used as a generic term to refer to any reader of this text. In addition, the term "synthesis tool" and "synthesis system" are used interchangeably in the text. Either of these refers to the program that reads in a Verilog RTL model and generates a gate level netlist.

In all the Verilog HDL descriptions that appear in this book, reserved words are in **boldface**. Occasionally ellipsis (. . .) is used in Verilog HDL source to indicate code that is not relevant to that discussion. Certain words such as `if` and `and` are written in `Courier` font so as to indicate their special meaning rather than their English meaning.

All examples that are described in this book have been synthesized using the ArchSyn synthesis system. Logic gates used in the synthesized netlists are described in Appendix B.

Acknowledgments

I gratefully acknowledge the following individuals for reviewing drafts of this book and for providing many constructive suggestions for improvement including many thought-provoking comments. I sincerely appreciate their time and effort spent in reviewing this book in spite of their busy work schedules.

- *i.* Cliff Cummings from Sunburst Design
- *ii.* Joe Pick from Synopsys
- *iii.* Doug Smith from VeriBest
- *iv.* Egbert Molenkamp from University of Twente, the Netherlands
- *v.* Carlos Roman, Jenjen Tiao, Jong Lee and Sriram Tyagarajan from Bell Labs, Lucent Technologies
- *vi.* Jim Vellenga and Ambar Sarkar from Viewlogic Systems

Thank you very much!

I would also like to thank Hao Nham for providing an excellent atmosphere here at Bell Labs and for encouraging me to pursue my extra-curricular activities (writing this book!) in addition to my regular work.

Of course, like my other books, this book would not be possible without the joy of my life, my family, my wife Geetha and my two rajahs, Arvind and Vinay, who provided me with the delight, pleasure and motivation to write yet another book!

J. Bhasker

August 1998

CHAPTER

1

BASICS

Verilog HDL is a hardware description language that can describe hardware not only at the gate level and the register-transfer level (RTL), but also at the algorithmic level. This makes translating a design described in Verilog HDL to logic gates a non-trivial process.

This chapter explains the basics involved in the mapping of a Verilog HDL model to logic gates.

1.1 What is Synthesis?

Synthesis is the process of constructing a gate level netlist from a register-transfer level model of a circuit described in Verilog HDL.[1] Figure 1-1 shows such a process. A synthesis system may as an intermediate step, generate a netlist that is comprised of register-transfer level blocks such as flip-flops, arithmetic-logic-units, and multiplexers, interconnected

1. This is the definition used in this book.

by wires. In such a case, a second program called the RTL module builder is necessary. The purpose of this builder is to build, or acquire from a library of predefined components, each of the required RTL blocks in the user-specified target technology.

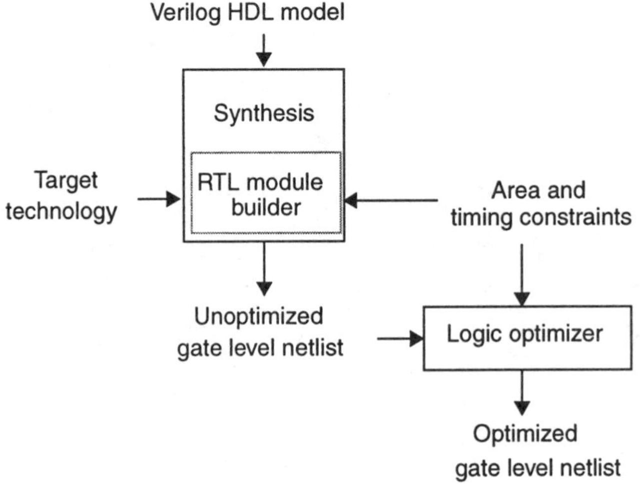

Figure 1-1 The synthesis process.

Having produced a gate level netlist, a logic optimizer reads in the netlist and optimizes the circuit for the user-specified area and timing constraints. These area and timing constraints may also be used by the module builder for appropriate selection or generation of RTL blocks.

In this book, we assume that the target netlist is at the gate level. The logic gates used in the synthesized netlists are described in Appendix B. The module building and logic optimization phases are not described in this book.

Figure 1-2 shows the basic elements of Verilog HDL and the elements used in hardware. A mapping mechanism or a construction mechanism has to be provided that translates the Verilog HDL elements into their corresponding hardware elements. Questions to ask are:

- How does a data type translate to hardware?
- How are constants mapped to logic values?
- How are statements translated to hardware?

The following sections discuss these mappings in more detail.

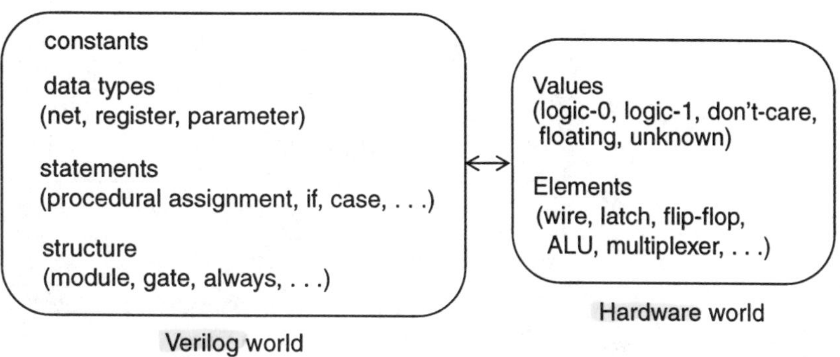

Figure 1-2 The two worlds of synthesis.

1.2 Synthesis in a Design Process

Verilog HDL is a hardware description language that allows a designer to model a circuit at different levels of abstraction, ranging from the gate level, register-transfer level, behavioral level to the algorithmic level. Thus a circuit can be described in many different ways, not all of which may be synthesizable. Compounding this is the fact that Verilog HDL was designed primarily as a simulation language and not as a language for synthesis. Consequently, there are many constructs in Verilog HDL that have no hardware counterpart, for example, the **$display** system call. Also there is no standardized subset of Verilog HDL for register-transfer level synthesis.

Because of these problems, different synthesis systems support different Verilog HDL subsets for synthesis. Since there is no single object in Verilog HDL that means a latch or a flip-flop, each synthesis system may provide different mechanisms to model a flip-flop or a latch. Each synthesis system therefore defines its own subset of Verilog HDL including its own modeling style.

Figure 1-3 shows a circuit that is described in many different ways using Verilog HDL. A synthesis system that supports synthesis of styles *A* and *B* may not support that of style *C*. This implies that typically synthesis models are non-portable across different synthesis systems. Style *D* may not be synthesizable at all.

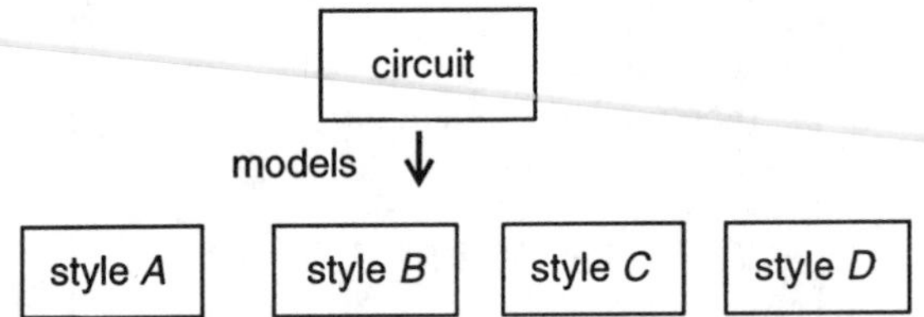

Figure 1-3 Same behavior, different styles.

This limitation creates a severe handicap because now the designer not only has to understand Verilog HDL, but also has to understand the synthesis-specific modeling style before a synthesizable model can be written. The typical design process shown in Figure 1-4 can not always be followed for Verilog HDL synthesis.

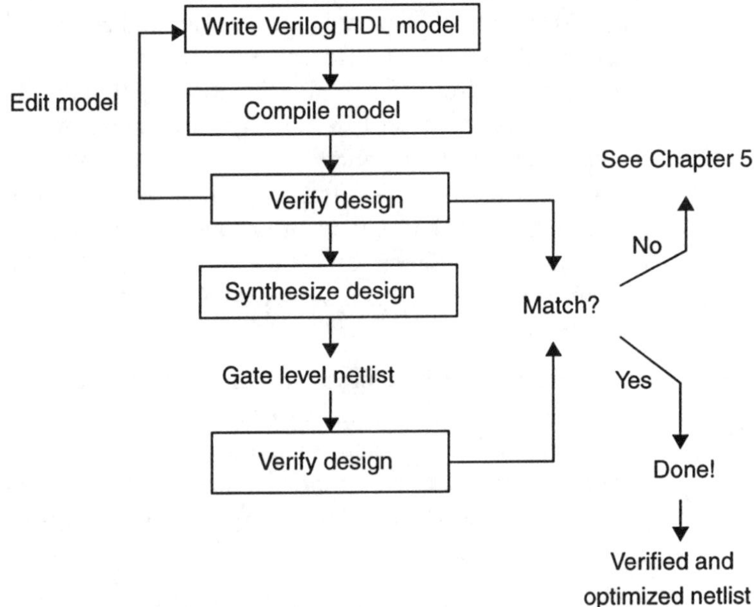

Figure 1-4 Typical design process.

The problem with this design process is that if the Verilog HDL model is written without knowing the synthesis modeling style (this assumes that the model is being written for synthesis; if not, then a non-synthesizable model may be perfectly okay), only during the synthesis phase will the designer learn about the synthesis-specific modeling restriction and style for synthesis. A model rewrite may be necessary at this point. Also a lot of time may have been wasted in the "Write Verilog HDL model" -> "Compile model" -> "Verify" -> "Edit model" loop. Instead, a more practical design process shown in Figure 1-5 has to be followed for Verilog HDL synthesis. The synthesis methodology checker is needed to ensure that the model being written is synthesizable. Note that this must be done within the first verification loop. In this way, after the verification results have been checked, a verified synthesizable model exists, which can then be synthesized.

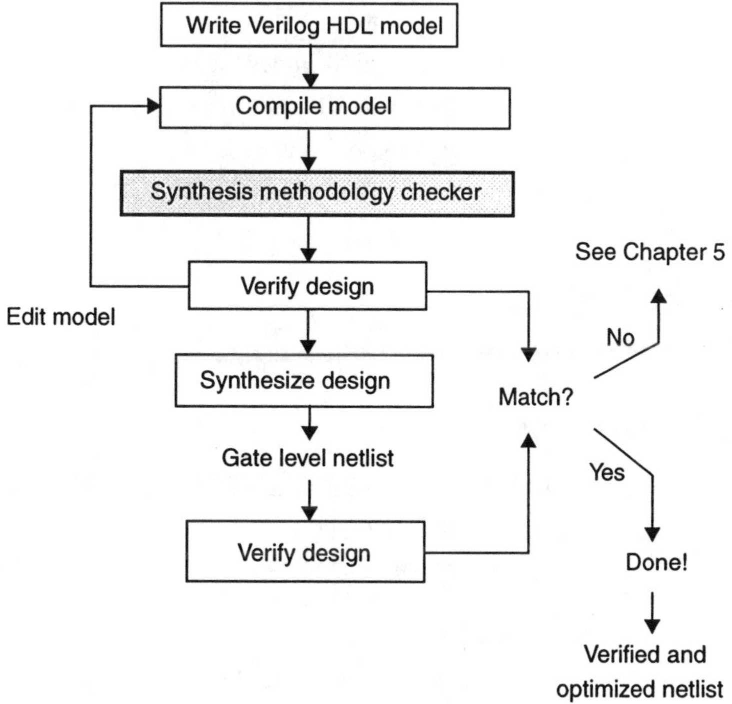

Figure 1-5 New design process.

1.3 Logic Value System

The common values used in modeling hardware are:

- logic-0
- logic-1
- high-impedance
- don't-care
- unknown

All these values are defined explicitly in Verilog HDL except for the don't-care value. A synthesis system treats the value x, when it is assigned to a variable, as a don't-care value. Here is the mapping between the Verilog HDL values and the hardware modeling values:

- 0 <--> logic-0
- 1 <--> logic-1
- z <--> high-impedance
- z <--> don't-care (in casex and casez statements)
- x <--> don't-care
- x <--> unknown

1.4 Bit-widths

1.4.1 Data Types

In Verilog HDL, a variable belongs to one of the two data types:

i. net data type

ii. register data type

Net Data Type

The size of a net is explicitly specified in a net declaration.

```
wire [4:0] Dak;                // A 5-bit wire net.
wor Ax;                        // 1-bit wor net.
```

When no size is explicitly specified in a net declaration, the default size is one bit.

Here are the different kinds of net data types that are supported for synthesis.

wire **wor** **wand** **tri** **supply0** **supply1**

The wire net is the most commonly used net type. When there are multiple drivers driving a wire net, the outputs of the drivers are shorted together. Here is an example.

```
module WireExample (BpW, Error, Wait, Valid, Clear);
  input Error, Wait, Valid, Clear;
  output BpW;
  wire BpW;
  assign BpW = Error & Wait;
  assign BpW = Valid | Clear;
endmodule
// Synthesized netlist is shown in Figure 1-6.
```

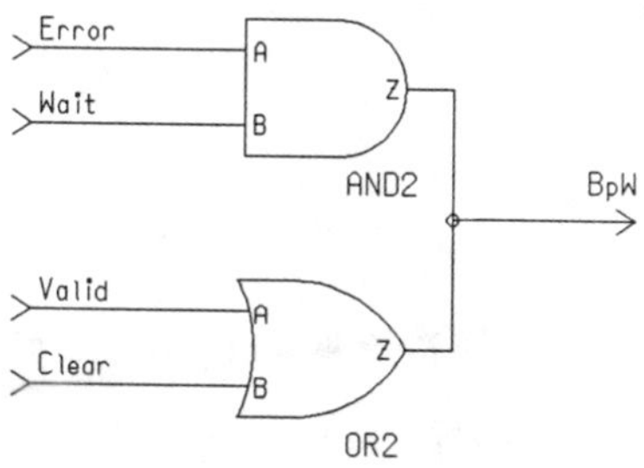

Figure 1-6 Multiple drivers driving a wire net.

The wor nets and wand nets are used when multiple driver resolution needs to be performed using or-logic and and-logic respectively. Upon synthesis, multiple drivers of such a net are connected together by an or gate (for a wor net) and by an and gate (for a wand net). Here is an example that shows this effect.

```
module UsesGates (BpW, BpR, Error, Wait, Clear);
  input Error, Wait, Clear;
  output BpW, BpR;
  wor BpW;
  wand BpR;

  assign BpW = Error & Wait;
  assign BpW = Valid | Clear;

  assign BpR = Error ^ Valid;
  assign BpR = ! Clear;
endmodule
// Synthesized netlist is shown in Figure 1-7.
```

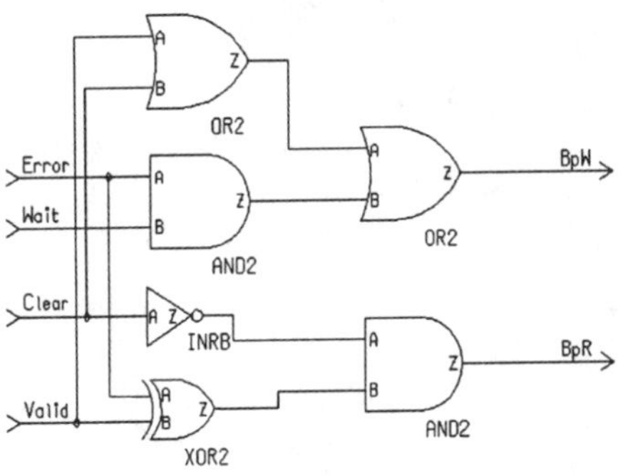

Figure 1-7 Wand net and wor net have multiple drivers.

The tri net synthesizes just like the wire net.

A supply0 net synthesizes to a wire that is permanently connected to 0 (logic-0), while a supply1 net synthesizes to a wire that is permanently connected to 1 (logic-1).

Register Data Type

The different kinds of register[1] types that are supported for synthesis are:

---

1. A variable of a register type does not necessarily imply a set of flip-flops in hardware. See next section.

```
reg        integer
```

A reg declaration explicitly specifies the size, that is, the corresponding number of bits of the variable in hardware. For example,

```
reg [1:25] Cpt;            // 25-bit variable.
reg Bxr;                   // 1-bit variable.
```

When no size is explicitly specified in a reg declaration, the default is one bit.

For an integer type, the maximum size is 32 bits and the number is assumed to be in 2's complement form. Optionally a synthesis system may perform data flow analysis of the model to determine the maximum size of an integer variable. For example,

```
wire [1:5] Brq, Rbu;
integer Arb;
. . .
Arb = Brq + Rbu;
```

Size of *Arb* is determined to be 6 bits. An adder of size 6 is sufficient. The leftmost bit is the carry bit.

The register types: time and real, are not supported for synthesis.

1.4.2 Constants

There are three kinds of constants in Verilog HDL: integer, real and string. Real and string constants are not supported for synthesis.

An integer constant can be written in either of the following two forms.

i. Simple decimal

ii. Base format

When an integer is written in a simple decimal form, it is interpreted as a signed number. The integer is represented in synthesis as 32 bits in 2's complement form. If an integer is written in the base format form, then the integer is treated as an unsigned number. If a size is explicitly specified for the integer, then the specified size is the number of bits used for the integer; if not, 32 bits is used for the size. Here are some examples.

```
30        Signed number, 32 bits
-2        Signed number, 32 bits in 2's complement
2'b10     Size of 2 bits
6'd-4     6-bit unsigned number (-4 is represented in
            2's complement using 6 bits)
'd-10     32-bit unsigned number (-10 is represented in
            2's complement using 32 bits)
```

1.4.3 Parameters

A parameter is a named constant. Since no size is allowed to be specified for a parameter, the size of the parameter is the same as the size of the constant itself.

```
parameter RED = -1, GREEN = 2;
parameter READY = 2'b01, BUSY = 2'b11, EXIT = 2'b10;
```

RED and *GREEN* are two 32-bit signed constants. *READY, BUSY* and *EXIT* are three parameters of size 2 bits each.

1.5 Value Holders for Hardware Modeling

The basic value holders in hardware are:

- wire
- flip-flop (an edge-triggered storage element)
- latch (a level-sensitive storage element)

A variable in Verilog HDL can either be of the net data type or the register data type. For synthesis, a variable of net type maps to a wire in hardware and a variable of the register type maps either to a wire or a storage element (flip-flop or latch) depending on the context under which the variable is assigned a value. Let us look at a variable of register type in more detail.

In Verilog HDL, a register variable retains its value through the entire simulation run, thus inferring memory. However, this is too general for synthesis. Here is an example of a variable that is used as a temporary and therefore need not be a candidate for a storage element.

```
wire Acr, Bar, Fra;        // A wire is a net type.
reg Trq, Sqp;              // A reg is a register type.
. . .
always @ (Bar or Acr or Fra)
begin1
  Trq = Bar & Acr;
  Sqp = Trq | Fra;
end
```

Variable *Trq* is assigned in the first statement and then used in the right-hand-side expression of the second statement. Verilog HDL semantics indicate that *Trq* retains its value through the entire simulation run. However, it is not necessary to store the value of *Trq* as a storage element in hardware, since it is assigned and used immediately. Figure 1-8 shows the logic generated.

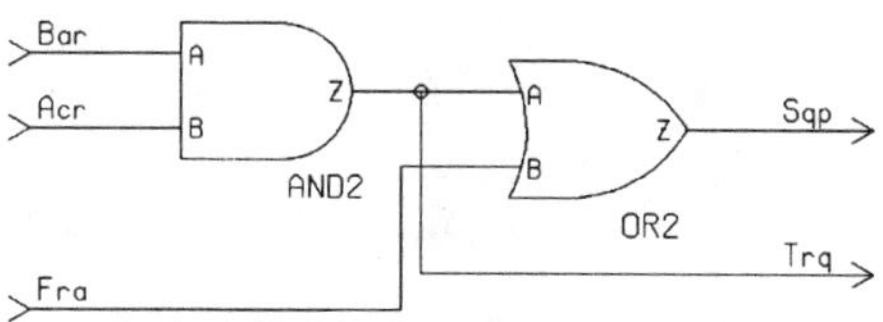

Figure 1-8 Variable *Trq* is a wire.

Let us look at another example. In this case, variable *Trq* is used before its assignment.

```
wire Acr, Bar, Fra;
reg Trq, Sqp;
. . .
always @ (Bar or Acr or Fra)
begin
  Sqp = Trq | Fra;
  Trq = Bar & Acr;
end
```

1. **begin** ... **end** is a sequential block; all statements that appear within it execute in sequence.

The semantics of this always statement is very clear in Verilog HDL. Whenever an event occurs on *Bar*, *Acr*, or *Fra* (those in the event list), execute the always statement. Since *Trq* is used before its assignment, *Trq* has to hold its value during repeated executions of the always statement, thus inferring memory. However, it is not clear how to build a latch for *Trq* because *Trq* is not assigned a value under the control of any condition. A synthesis system may not create a latch in this case and may generate the circuit shown in Figure 1-9. Variable *Trq* is synthesized to a wire again. However, for functionality to match between the Verilog HDL model and the synthesized netlist, *Trq* must also be in the event list of the always statement. More of this is discussed in Chapter 5.

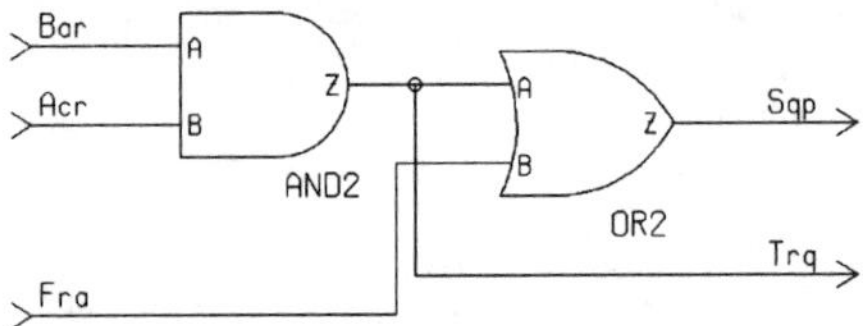

Figure 1-9 No latch for variable *Trq*.

Here is an example where a latch is inferred for a variable.

```
wire Sat, Ant;
reg Fox, Sout;
. . .
always @ (Sat or Ant)
begin
  if (! Sat)
    Fox = Ant;

  Sout = ! Fox;
end
```

The variable *Fox* is not assigned in the else-branch of the conditional statement. Consequently, a latch is inferred for *Fox* since it needs to retain its value when *Sat* is true. The circuit synthesized in shown in Figure 1-10.

How is a flip-flop inferred? It depends on the modeling style being followed and the context under which a variable is assigned a value. This

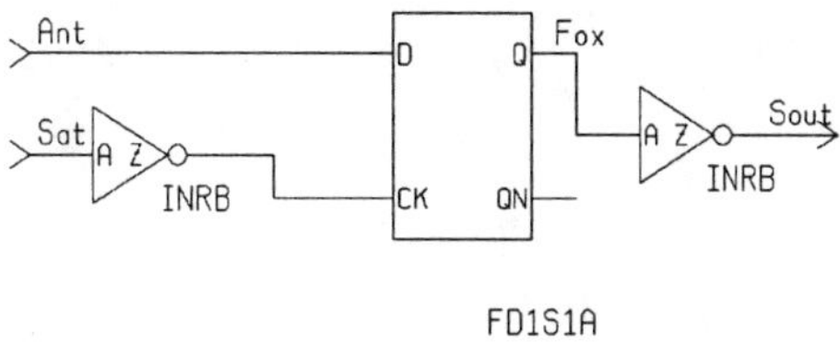

Figure 1-10 Variable *Fox* is a latch.

and other examples for flip-flop and latch inferencing are discussed in the next chapter. A memory in hardware can be modeled as an array of flip-flops or latches.

❑

CHAPTER

2

VERILOG CONSTRUCTS TO GATES

The previous chapter described the mapping from Verilog HDL types and constants to hardware. This chapter describes the mapping of statements in Verilog HDL to logic gates in hardware. It also explains how operators, expressions and assignments are mapped to hardware. Each section of this chapter describes a particular synthesis construct or feature in a cookbook style for ease of reading and understanding. Most of the synthesized netlists are not optimized and do not represent minimal hardware.

2.1 Continuous Assignment Statement

A continuous assignment statement represents, in hardware, logic that is derived from the expression on the right-hand-side of the assignment statement driving the net that appears on the left-hand-side of the assignment. The target of a continuous assignment is always a net driven by combinational logic.

Here is an example.

```
module Continuous (StatIn, StatOut);
  input StatIn;
  output StatOut;

  assign StatOut = ~ StatIn; // Continuous assignment.
endmodule
// Synthesized netlist is shown in Figure 2-1.
```

Figure 2-1 Combinational circuit from continuous assignment statement.

The continuous assignment statement describes an inverter that has its input connected to *StatIn* and whose output is *StatOut*. Delays, if any, specified in a continuous assignment statement are usually ignored by a synthesis system. For example, in the continuous assignment:

```
assign #2 EffectiveAB = DriverA | DriverB;
```

the delay #2 is ignored for synthesis.

2.2 Procedural Assignment Statement

A procedural assignment statement represents, in hardware, logic that is derived from the expression on the right-hand-side of the assignment statement driving the variable that appears on the left-hand-side of the assignment. Note that procedural assignments can appear only within an always statement[1].

There are two kinds of procedural assignment statements:

i. Blocking

ii. Non-blocking

2.2.1 Blocking Procedural Assignment

Here is an example of a blocking procedural assignment statement.

```
module Blocking (Preset, Count);
  input [0:2] Preset;
  output [3:0] Count;
  reg [3:0] Count;

  always @ (Preset)
    Count = Preset + 1;
    // Blocking procedural assignment.
endmodule
// Synthesized netlist is shown in Figure 2-2.
```

The blocking procedural assignment statement describes an adder that takes *Preset* and the integer 1 as inputs and places the result in the variable *Count*.

1. Procedural assignments can appear within an initial statement as well; however an initial statement is not supported for synthesis.

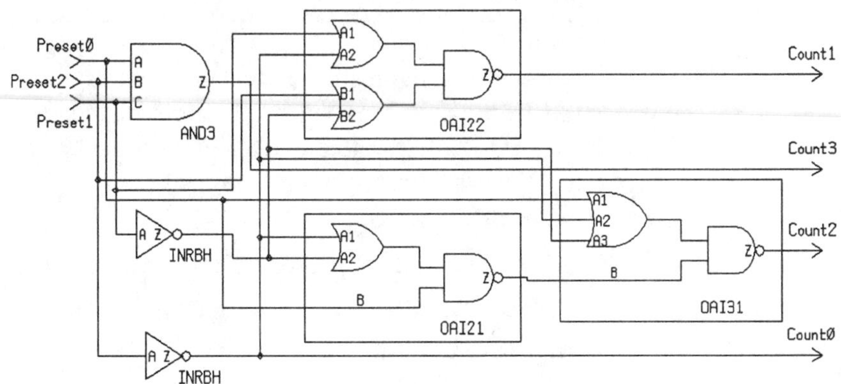

Figure 2-2 Combinational circuit from blocking procedural assignment.

2.2.2 Non-blocking Procedural Assignment

Here is an example of an non-blocking procedural assignment.

```
module NonBlocking (RegA, Mask, RegB);
  input [3:0] RegA, Mask;
  output [3:0] RegB;
  reg [3:0] RegB;

  always @ (RegA or Mask)
    RegB <= RegA & Mask;
    // Non-blocking procedural assignment.
endmodule
// Synthesized netlist is shown in Figure 2-3.
```

The blocking or non-blocking nature of an assignment does not cause any change to the combinational logic generated from the assignment statement itself, but affects the use of the resultant value later on.

A good recommendation to follow is to use blocking assignments for modeling combinational logic and to use non-blocking assignments for modeling sequential logic; more on this is described in later sections.

The subtle differences between a blocking and a non-blocking procedural assignment are explored in section 2.18.

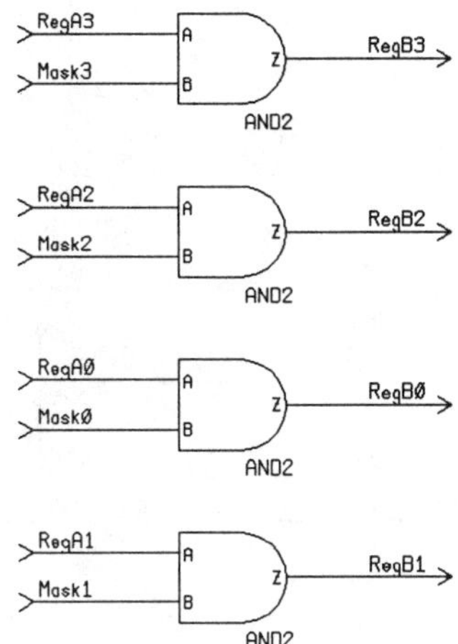

Figure 2-3 Combinational logic from non-blocking procedural assignment.

2.2.3 Target of Assignment

The target of a procedural assignment is synthesized into a wire, a flip-flop, or a latch, depending on the context under which the assignment appears in the Verilog HDL model. For example, if the previously described non-blocking procedural assignment statement appeared, say, under the control of a clock as shown in the following example, then the target is synthesized as a flip-flop.

```
module Target (Clk, RegA, RegB, Mask);
  input Clk;
  input [3:0] RegA, Mask;
  output [3:0] RegB;
  reg [3:0] RegB;

  always @ (posedge Clk)
    RegB <= RegA & Mask;
endmodule
// Synthesized netlist is shown in Figure 2-4.
```

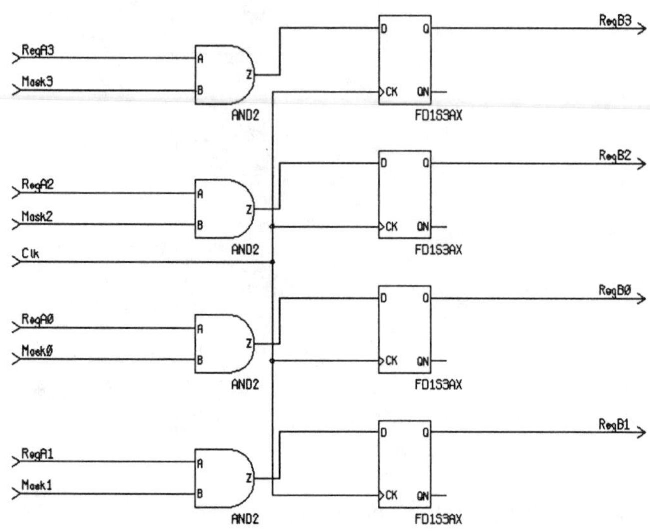

Figure 2-4 Target of an assignment is a flip-flop.

2.2.4 Assignment Restrictions

Any kind of delay, delay control or intra-statement delay, specified in a procedural assignment (blocking or non-blocking) is ignored by a synthesis system. This can potentially lead to a functional mismatch between the design model and its synthesized netlist.

```
#5 RegB <= RegA & Mask;
  // Delay control #5 is ignored.
RegB = #2 RegA & Mask;
  // Intra-statement delay #2 is ignored.
```

There is another restriction on using both blocking and non-blocking assignments in a single model for synthesis.

```
A target cannot be assigned using a blocking assignment
and a non-blocking assignment.
```

What this means is that if a target is assigned using a blocking (or a non-blocking) assignment, then the same target can only be assigned again using a blocking (or a non-blocking) assignment. Here is an example.

```
Count = Preset + 1;
. . .
Count <= Mask; // This is illegal since Count is
      // previously assigned using a blocking assignment.
```

2.3 Logical Operators

The logical operators get directly mapped onto primitive logic gates in hardware. Here is a model of a full-adder using continuous assignment statements.

```
module FullAdder (A, B, CarryIn, Sum, CarryOut);
  input A, B, CarryIn;
  output Sum, CarryOut;

  assign Sum = (A ^ B) ^ CarryIn;
  assign CarryOut = (A & B) | (B & CarryIn) |
                    (A & CarryIn);
endmodule
// Synthesized netlist is shown in Figure 2-5.
```

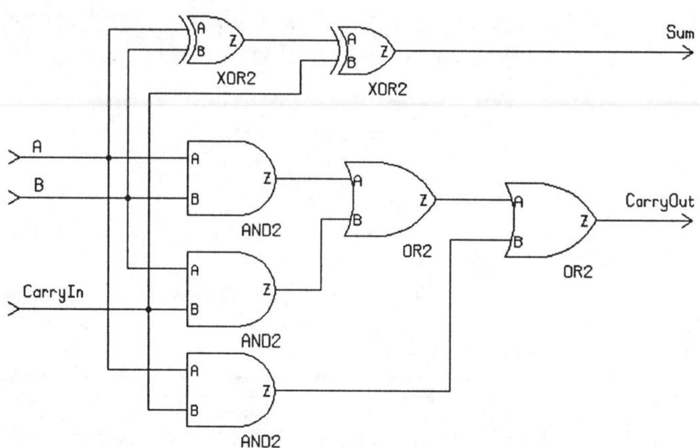

Figure 2-5 Logical operators map to primitive logic gates.

2.4 Arithmetic Operators

In Verilog HDL, a reg type is interpreted as an unsigned number and an integer type is interpreted as a signed number in 2's complement form with the rightmost bit as the least significant bit. Thus, to synthesize an unsigned arithmetic operator, the reg type is used. To get a signed arithmetic operator, the integer type is used.

The net type is interpreted as unsigned numbers.

2.4.1 Unsigned Arithmetic

Here is an example that uses an arithmetic operator on unsigned numbers.

```
module UnsignedAdder (Arb, Bet, Lot);
  input [2:0] Arb, Bet;
  output [2:0] Lot;

  assign Lot = Arb + Bet;
endmodule
// Synthesized netlist is shown in Figure 2-6.
```

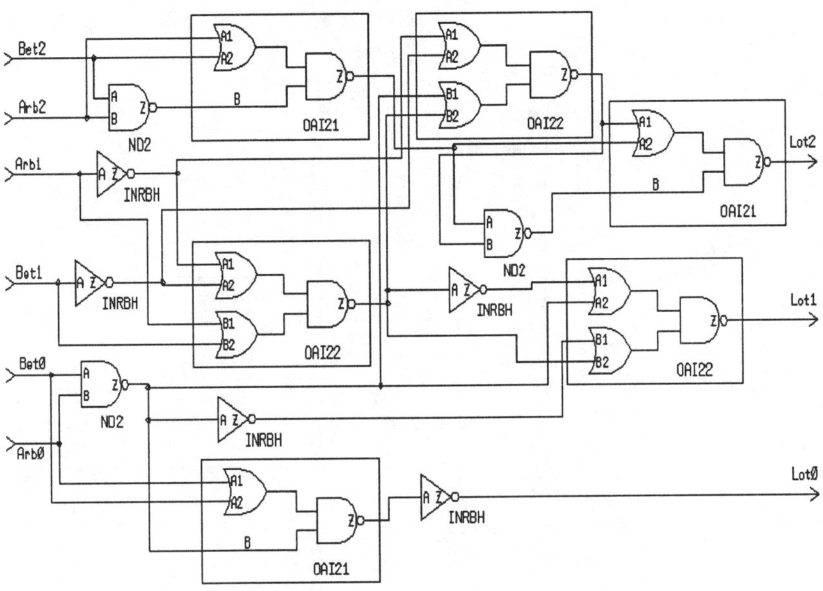

Figure 2-6 A 3-bit adder.

In this example, a 3-bit adder is being modeled. The number system for the operands is unsigned since they are of the net type. The leftmost bit is the most significant bit.

2.4.2 Signed Arithmetic

Here is an example in which the operands are signed numbers. This is achieved by using the integer type.

```
module SignedAdder (Arb, Bet, Lot);
  input [1:0] Arb, Bet;
  output [2:0] Lot;
  reg [2:0] Lot;

  always @ (Arb or Bet)
  begin: LABEL_A
    // A sequential block requires a label if local
    // declarations are present.
    integer ArbInt, BetInt;
```

```
        ArbInt = - Arb; // Store negative number just to show
             //that the + is operating on signed operands.
        BetInt = Bet;
        Lot = ArbInt + BetInt;
      end
    endmodule
    // Synthesized netlist is shown in Figure 2-7.
```

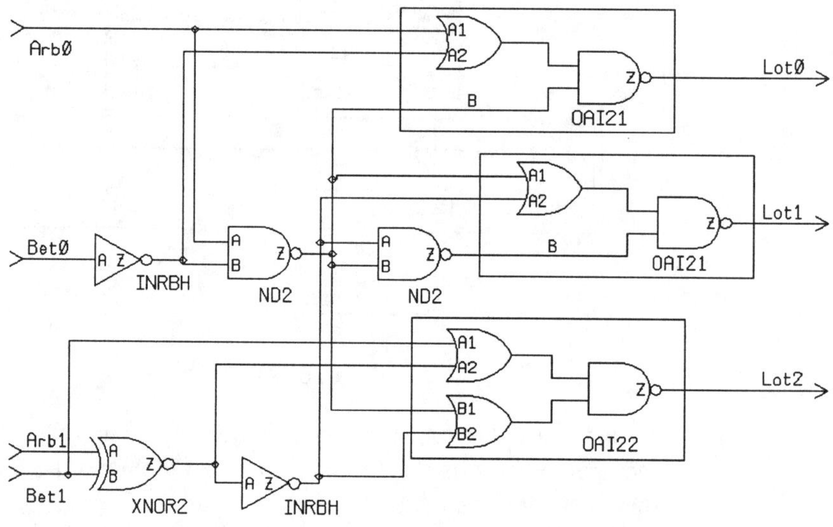

Figure 2-7 Signed adder.

Note that the adder logic with signed operands is the same as that with unsigned operands since the signed values are represented in 2's complement form.

2.4.3 Modeling a Carry

It is natural to model a carry by simply using the result size to be one bit larger than the largest of the two operands. Alternatively, a concatenation could also be used as the target of an assignment with the carry bit explicitly specified. Here are examples of these.

```
wire [3:0] CdoBus, Sum;
wire [4:0] OneUp;
```

```
wire Bore;
. . .
assign OneUp = CdoBus + 1;
assign {Bore, Sum} = CdoBus - 2;
```

In the first continuous assignment, the result of the operation is five bits and *OneUp*[4] has the carry bit. If *OneUp* were declared as:

```
wire [3:0] OneUp;
```

then the carry bit would have been lost. In the second continuous assignment, *Bore* has the borrow bit of the subtraction operation.

2.5 Relational Operators

The relational operators supported for synthesis are:

```
>, <, <=, >=
```

Relational operators can be modeled similar to arithmetic operators. In this case, the logic produced from synthesis is different depending on whether unsigned or signed numbers are being compared. If variables of a reg type or a net type are compared, an unsigned relational operator is synthesized. If integer variables are compared, then a signed relational operator is synthesized. Here is an example of a relational operator that is used with unsigned numbers.

```
module GreaterThan (A, B, Z);
  input [3:0] A, B;
  output Z;

  assign Z = A[1:0] > B[3:2];
  // Variables A and B are of net type.
endmodule
// Synthesized netlist is shown in Figure 2-8.
```

Here is an example of synthesizing a signed relational operator. In this case, the operands for the relational operator are integer variables.

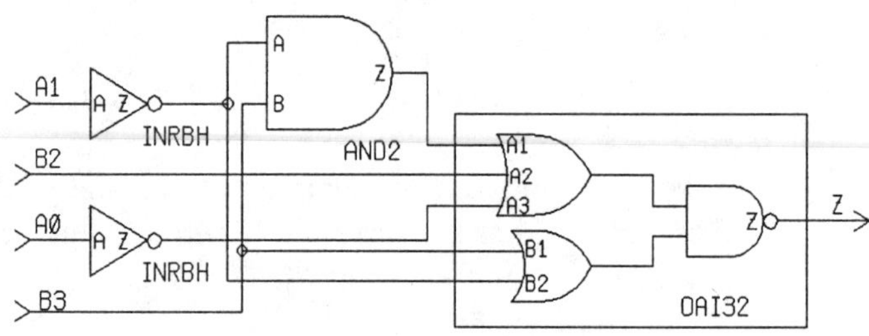

Figure 2-8 Unsigned ">" relational operator.

```
module LessThanEquals (ArgA, ArgB, ResultZ);
  input [2:0] ArgA, ArgB;
  output ResultZ;
  reg ResultZ;
  integer ArgAInt, ArgBInt;

  always @ (ArgA or ArgB)
  begin
    ArgAInt = - ArgA;
    ArgBInt = - ArgB;
    // Store negative values just to show that the
    // comparison is on signed numbers.
    ResultZ = ArgAInt <= ArgBInt;
  end
endmodule
// Synthesized netlist is shown in Figure 2-9.
```

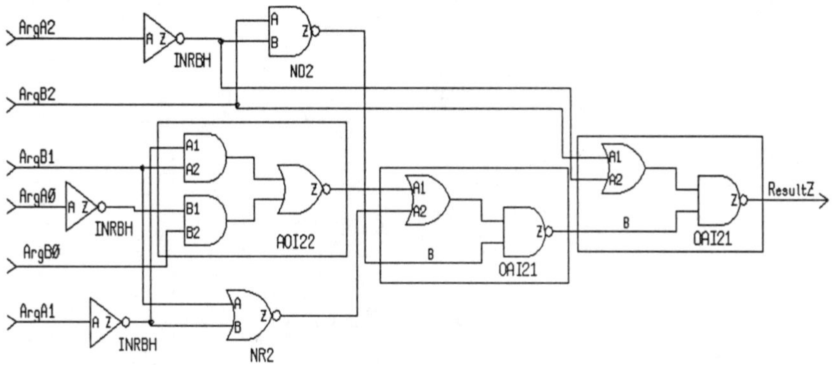

Figure 2-9 Signed "<=" relational operator.

2.6 Equality Operators

The equality operators supported for synthesis are:

```
==, !=
```

The operators === (case equality) and !== (case inequality) are not supported for synthesis.

Equality operators are modeled similar to arithmetic operators in terms of whether signed or unsigned comparison is to be made. Here is an example that uses signed numbers. Note that in this case, the operands of the equality operator are of integer type because values of this type represent signed numbers.

```
module NotEquals (A, B, Z);
  input [0:3] A, B;
  output Z;
  reg Z;

  always @ (A or B)
  begin: DF_LABEL
    integer IntA, IntB;

    IntA = A;
```

```
    IntB = B;
    Z = IntA != IntB;
  end
endmodule
// Synthesized netlist is shown in Figure 2-10.
```

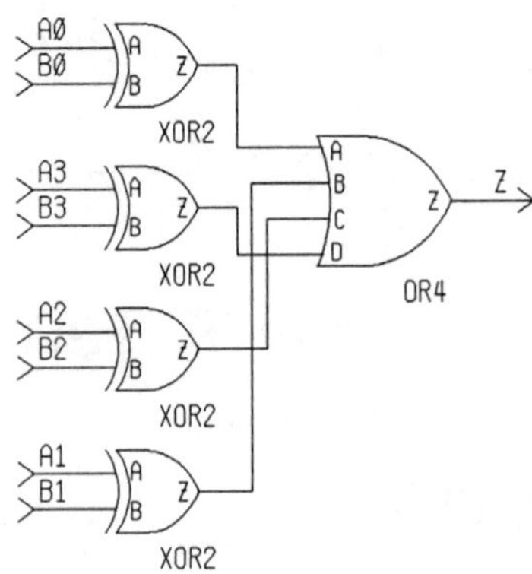

Figure 2-10 Signed "!=" relational operator.

2.7 Shift Operators

Verilog HDL synthesis supports the left shift (<<) and the right shift (>>) operators. The vacated bits are filled with 0. The right operand, which is the amount of shift, may either be a constant or a variable. In both cases, combinational logic is produced. When shifting by a constant, simple rewiring is performed. When shifting by a variable, a general-purpose shifter is synthesized. This is shown in the following examples.

```
module ConstantShift (DataMux, Address);
  input [0:3] DataMux;
  output [0:5] Address;

  assign Address = (~ DataMux) << 2;
endmodule
// Synthesized netlist is shown in Figure 2-11.
```

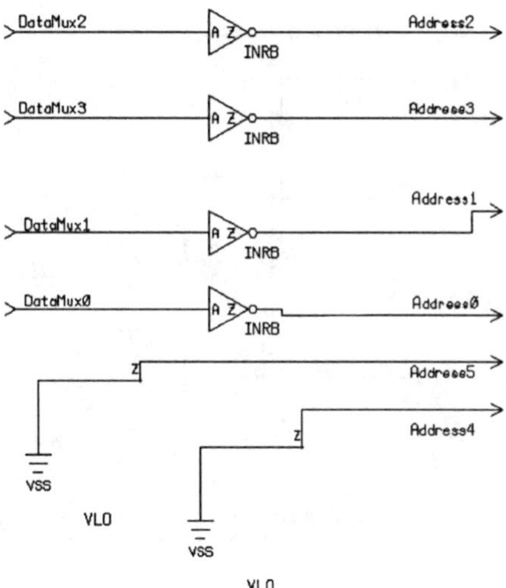

Figure 2-11 Constant shift.

```
module VariableShift (MemDataReg, Amount, InstrReg);
  input [0:2] MemDataReg;
  input [0:1] Amount;
  output [0:2] InstrReg;

  assign InstrReg = MemDataReg >> Amount;
endmodule
// Synthesized netlist is shown in Figure 2-12.
```

As per Verilog HDL rules, when performing the left shift operation in module *ConstantShift*, the shifted bits from *DataMux* are not discarded but simply move into the higher order bits of *Address*. If *Address* were the same size as *DataMux*, then the high-order bits get shifted out and discarded.

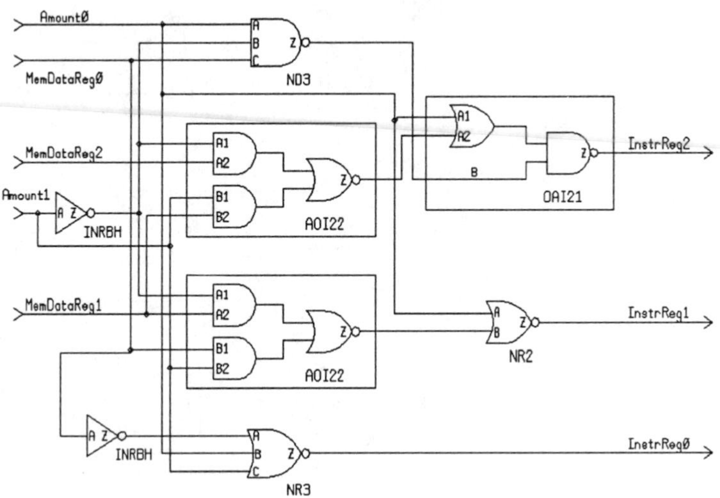

Figure 2-12 Variable shift.

2.8 Vector Operations

This example shows that vector operands can be used in expressions. The four bits of *A* are and'ed with the four bits of *B*, the result of which is or'ed with the four bits of *C*. The result is assigned (starting with the rightmost bit) to the target net *RFile*.

```
module VectorOperations (A, B, C, RFile);
  input [3:0] A, B, C;
  output [3:0] RFile;

  assign RFile = (A & B) | C;
endmodule
// Synthesized netlist is shown in Figure 2-13.
```

Here is another example where the operands of a logical operator are vectors. In such a case, a series of logic gates to cover the range of the vector are produced.

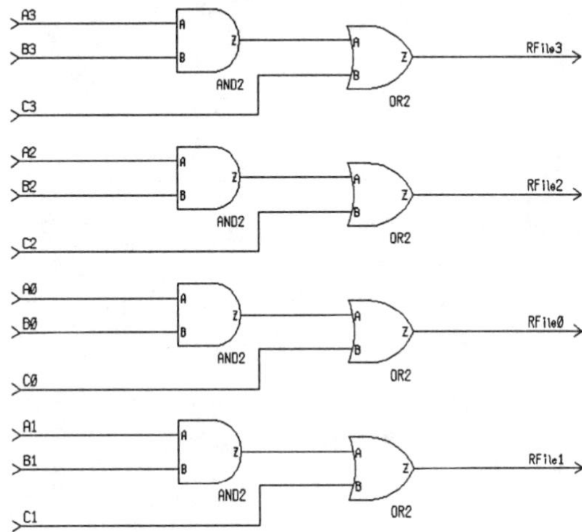

Figure 2-13 Vector operations.

```
module VectorOperands (Bi, Stdy, Tap);
  input [0:3] Bi, Stdy;
  output [0:3] Tap;

  assign Tap = Bi ^ Stdy;
endmodule
// Synthesized netlist is shown in Figure 2-14.
```

Four exclusive-or gates are synthesized since each operand in the right-hand-side is of size 4.

In the above examples on continuous assignments, there is a one-to-one correlation between a continuous assignment statement and its synthesized logic. This is because a continuous assignment implicitly describes the structure.

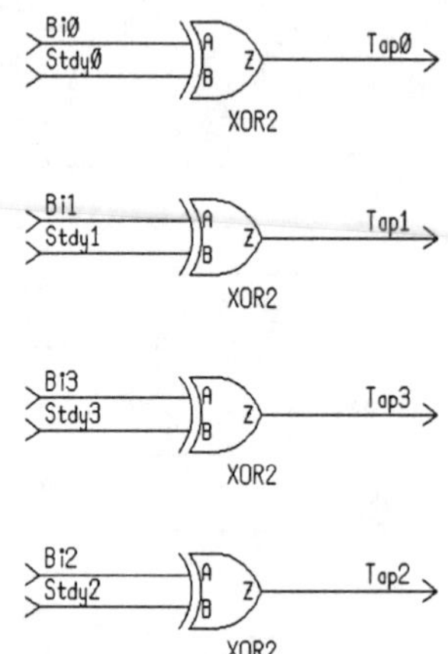

Figure 2-14 A bank of logic gates.

2.9 Part-selects

Operations using part-selects can be used in a model. Here is an example.

```
module PartSelect (A, C, ZCat);
  input [3:0] A, C;
  output [3:0] ZCat;

  assign ZCat[2:0] = {A[2], C[3:2]};
endmodule
// Synthesized netlist is shown in Figure 2-15.
```

ZCat[2:0] and *C*[3:2] are examples of part-selects. Non-constant part-selects are not supported in Verilog HDL.

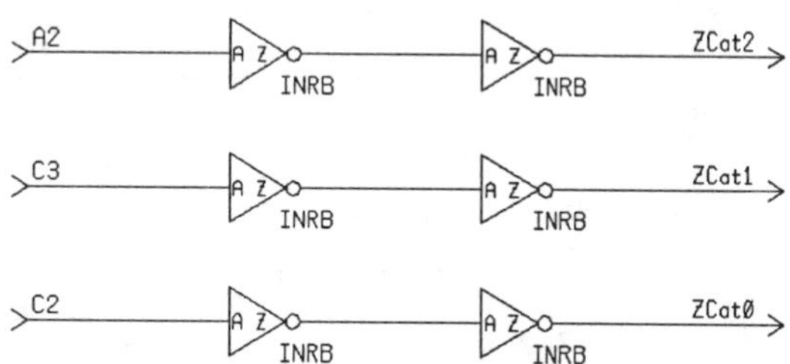

Figure 2-15 Part-select example.

2.10 Bit-selects

A bit-select can be a constant index or a non-constant index.

2.10.1 Constant Index

Here is an example that uses constant values for bit-select indices.

```
module ConstantIndex (A, C, Reg_File, ZCat);
  input [3:0] A, C;
  input [3:0] Reg_File;
  output [3:0] ZCat;

  assign ZCat[3:1] = {A[2], C[3:2]};
  assign ZCat[0] = Reg_File[3];
endmodule
// Synthesized netlist is shown in Figure 2-16.
```

A[2], *ZCat*[0] and *Reg_File*[3] are examples of bit-selects. The concatenation operator, { }, is used to generate a bigger array.

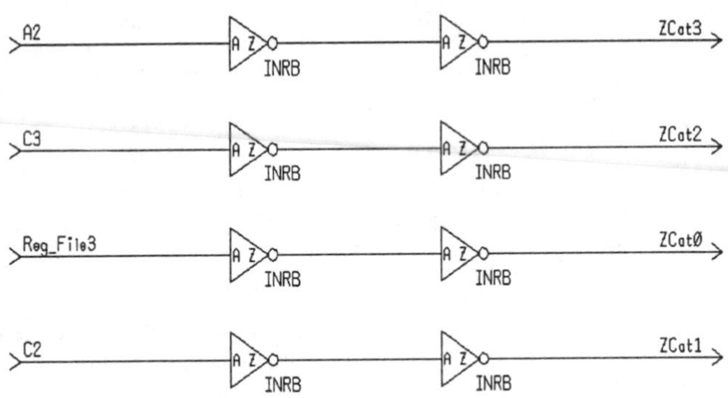

Figure 2-16 Constant bit-select.

2.10.2 Non-constant Index in Expression

It is possible to use a non-constant as an index in a bit-select as shown in the following model.

```
module NonComputeRight (Data, Index, Dout);
  input [0:3] Data;
  input [1:2] Index;
  output Dout;

  assign Dout = Data [Index];
endmodule
// Synthesized netlist is shown in Figure 2-17.
```

In this case, a multiplexer is generated as shown in the synthesized netlist.

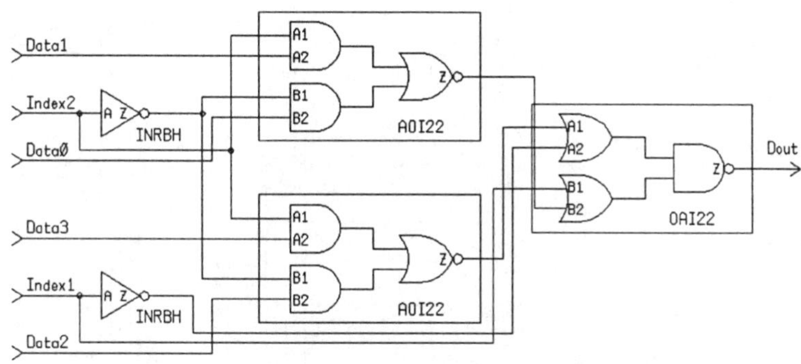

Figure 2-17 Non-constant bit-select generates a multiplexer.

2.10.3 Non-constant Index in Target

Here is another example of a non-constant bit-select; this time it is used on the left-hand-side of an assignment. A decoder is synthesized for this behavior.

```
module NonComputeLeft (Mem, Store, Addr);
  output [7:0] Mem;
  input Store;
  input [1:3] Addr;

  assign Mem [Addr] = Store;
endmodule
// Synthesized netlist is shown in Figure 2-18.
```

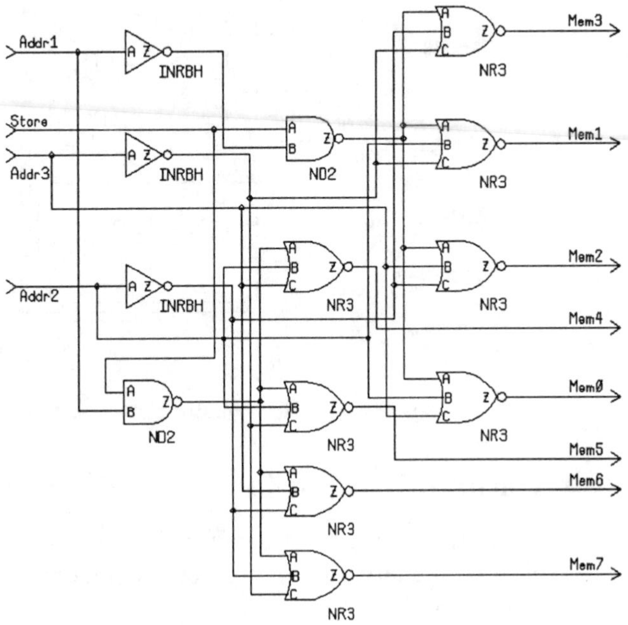

Figure 2-18 A decoder generated from a non-constant bit-select.

2.11 Conditional Expression

A conditional expression selects between two expressions according to the value of a condition.

```
<condition> ? <expression1> : <expression2>
```

If the condition is true, select the first expression, else select the second. Here is an example.

```
module ConditionalExpression (StartXM, ShiftVal,
                              Reset, StopXM);
  input StartXM, ShiftVal, Reset;
  output StopXM;
```

```
  assign StopXM = (! Reset) ? StartXM ^ ShiftVal :
                              StartXM | ShiftVal;
endmodule
// Synthesized netlist is shown in Figure 2-19.
```

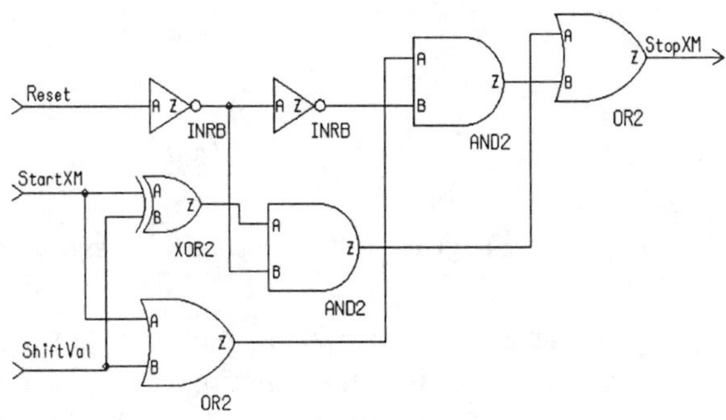

Figure 2-19 Logic generated from a conditional expression.

2.12 Always Statement

An always statement is used to model the procedural behavior of a circuit. Here is an example of an always statement that contains procedural assignment statements.

```
module EvenParity (A, B, C, D, Z);
  input A, B, C, D;
  output Z;
  reg Z, Temp1, Temp2;

  always @(A or B or C or D)
  begin
    Temp1 = A ^ B;
    Temp2 = C ^ D;
    Z = Temp1 ^ Temp2;
    // Note that the temporaries are really not
    // required. They are used here to illustrate the
    // sequential behavior of the statements within
    // the sequential block.
  end
```

```
endmodule
// Synthesized netlist is shown in Figure 2-20.
```

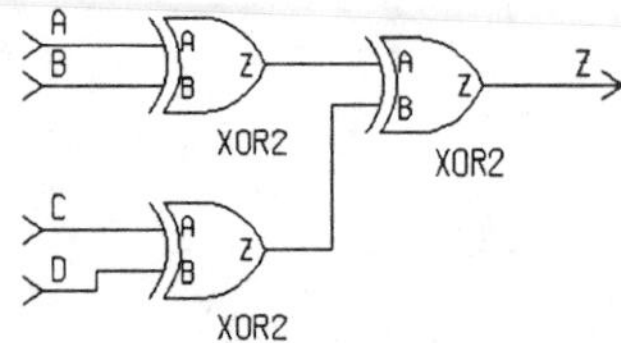

Figure 2-20 Procedural assignment statements.

All variables whose values are read in the always statement must appear in the event list (the parenthesized list following the "@" symbol); otherwise the functionality of the synthesized netlist may not match that of the design model. Here is a simple example that illustrates this point.

```
module AndBehavior (Z, A, B);
  input A, B;
  output Z;
  reg Z;

  always @ (B)
    Z = A & B;
endmodule
// Synthesized netlist is shown in Figure 2-21.
```

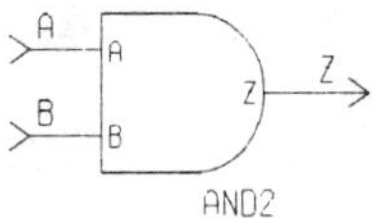

Figure 2-21 Incomplete event list.

The semantics of the always statement specifies that whenever an event occurs on *B*, the assignment is to be executed and *Z* gets a value. If any events occur on *A*, this has no impact on the value of *Z*. However, the synthesized netlist of the above module, shown in Figure 2-21, shows an and gate. Here any time *A* or *B* changes, the value of *Z* is updated. Hence a functional mismatch occurs. A synthesis system usually would issue a warning about such missing variables in the event list.

A good practice is to include all variables read in the always statement in the event list; this is true only when modeling combinational logic. When modeling sequential logic, a different kind of event list is required; this is described later.

A variable declared within an always statement holds a temporary value and does not necessarily infer a unique wire in hardware as the following example shows.

```
module VariablesAreTemporaries (A, B, C, D, Z);
  input A, B, C, D;
  output Z;
  reg Z;

  always @ (A or B or C or D)
  begin: VAR_LABEL
    integer T1, T2;

    T1 = A & B;
    T2 = C & D;
    T1 = T1 | T2;
    Z = ~ T1;
  end
endmodule
// Synthesized netlist is shown in Figure 2-22.
```

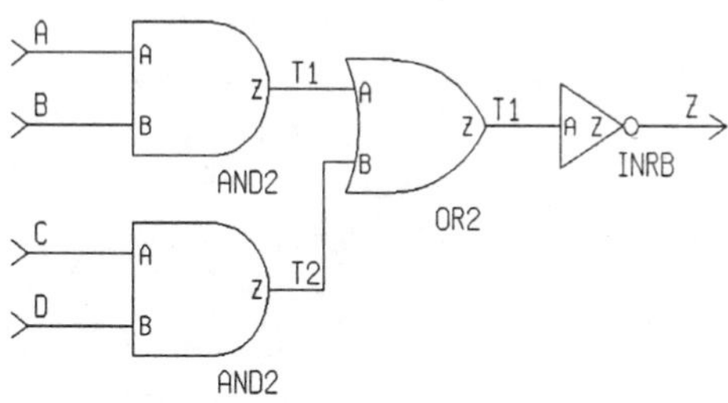

Figure 2-22 One variable can represent many wires.

In the synthesized netlist, the output of the *AND2* gate is the variable *T1*; so is the output of the *OR2* gate. In this example, each assignment to the integer variable infers a unique wire.

2.13 If Statement

An `if` statement represents logic that is conditionally controlled. Here is an example.

```
module SelectOneOf (A, B, Z);
  input [1:0] A, B;
  output [1:0] Z;
  reg [1:0] Z;

  always @ (A or B)
    if (A > B)
      Z = A;
    else
      Z = B;
endmodule
// Synthesized netlist is shown in Figure 2-23.
```

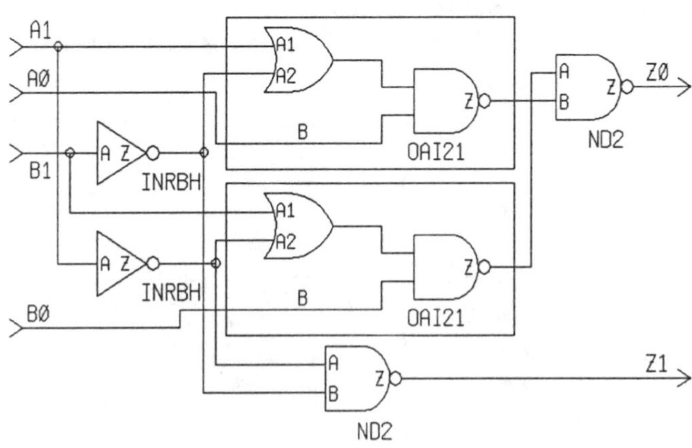

Figure 2-23 Logic derived from an `if` statement.

Here is another example of an `if` statement.

```
module SimpleALU (Ctrl, A, B, Z);
  input Ctrl;
  input [0:1] A, B;
  output [0:1] Z;
  reg [0:1] Z;

  always @ (Ctrl or A or B)
    if (Ctrl)
      Z = A & B;
    else
      Z = A | B;
endmodule
// Synthesized netlist is shown in Figure 2-24.
```

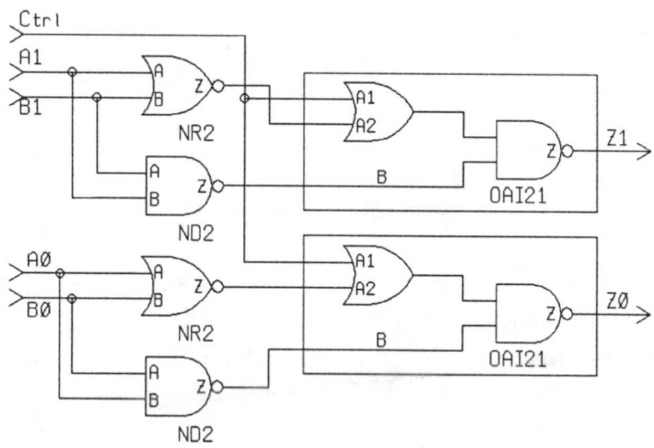

Figure 2-24 Conditional selection of operations.

2.13.1 Inferring Latches from If Statements

Consider the always statement in the following module.

```
module Increment (Phy, Ones, Z);
  input Phy;
  input [0:1] Ones;
  output [0:2] Z;
  reg [0:2] Z;
```

```
    always @ (Phy or Ones)
      if (Phy)
        Z = Ones + 1;

  endmodule
  // Synthesized netlist is shown in Figure 2-25.
```

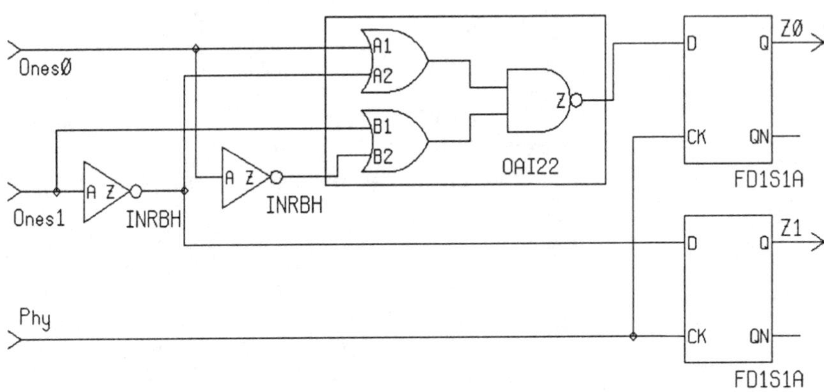

Figure 2-25 A variable is synthesized as a latch.

The semantics of the always statement specifies that every time an event occurs on *Phy* or *Ones* (variables present in the event list), the `if` statement executes and the variable *Z* gets the value of *Ones* incremented by 1 if *Phy* is a 1. If *Phy* is a 0, the value in *Z* is retained; this is done using latches.

A general rule for latch inferencing is that if a variable is not assigned in all possible executions of an always statement (for example, when a variable is not assigned in all branches of an `if` statement), then a latch is inferred.

Here is another example of a variable that is not assigned in all branches of an `if` statement.

```
module Compute (Marks, Grade);
  input [1:4] Marks;
  output [0:1] Grade;
  reg [0:1] Grade;
```

```
    parameter FAIL = 1, PASS = 2, EXCELLENT = 3;

    always @ (Marks)
      if (Marks < 5)
        Grade = FAIL;
      else if ((Marks >= 5) & (Marks < 10))
        Grade = PASS;
endmodule
// Synthesized netlist is shown in Figure 2-26.
```

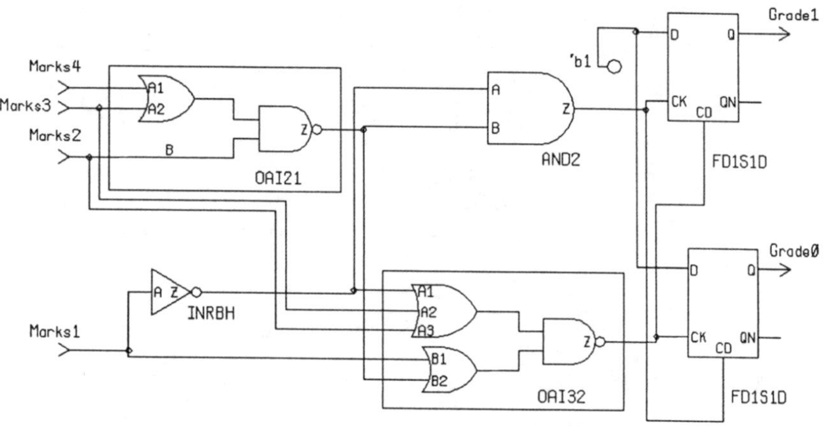

Figure 2-26 A variable is inferred as a latch.

In this example, what should be the value of *Grade* if *Marks* has the value 12? It may be intended to be a don't care, but from the language semantics viewpoint, the variable *Grade* retains its last value, since no value is assigned to the variable explicitly when *Marks* has the value 12. Therefore a latch is inferred for *Grade* in keeping with the simulation semantics of a reg variable.

Arithmetic operations as conditional expressions, as in the previous example, should be avoided when inferring latches since there is a very high probability of race condition between the conditionals in the synthesized netlist; this might cause the latched value in the synthesized netlist to differ from that in the Verilog HDL model.

If a variable is not assigned in all branches of an `if` statement, and the intention is not to infer a latch, then the variable must be assigned a value explicitly in all the branches of the `if` statement. If the previous example is modified by specifying the assignment to the variable in all branches, the following program is obtained.

```
module ComputeNoLatch (Marks, Grade);
  input [1:4] Marks;
  output [0:1] Grade;
  reg [0:1] Grade;
  parameter FAIL = 1, PASS = 2, EXCELLENT = 3;

  always @ (Marks)
    if (Marks < 5)
      Grade = FAIL;
    else if ((Marks >= 5) && (Marks < 10))
      Grade = PASS;
    else
      Grade = EXCELLENT;
endmodule
// Synthesized netlist is shown in Figure 2-27.
```

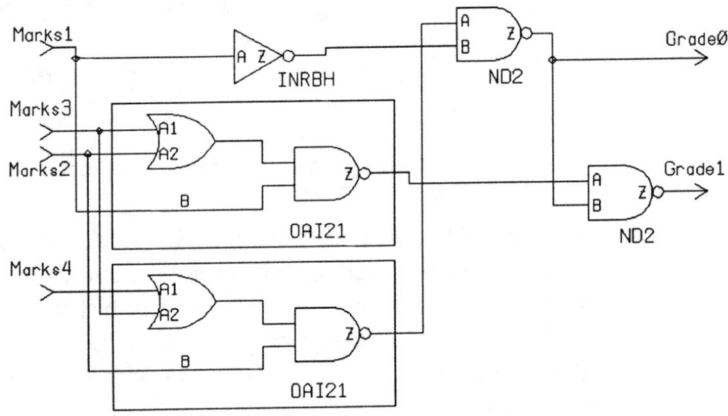

Figure 2-27 Variable GRADE is not a latch.

In this case, variable *GRADE* is not a latch because it is assigned a value in all branches of the `if` statement.

2.14 Case Statement

A case statement is of the form:

```
case ( <case_expression> )
  <case_itemA1>, <case_itemA2>, . . .: <statementA>
  <case_itemB1>, <case_itemB2>, . . .: <statementB>
  . . .
  default                            : <statementD>
endcase
```

The first branch that has a case item whose value matches the value of the case expression is selected. A case item may be a constant or a variable.

Here is an example of a case statement.

```
module ALU (Op, A, B, Z);
  input [1:2] Op;
  input [0:1] A, B;
  output [0:1] Z;
  reg [0:1] Z;

  parameter ADD = 'b00, SUB = 'b01, MUL = 'b10,
            DIV = 'b11;

  always @(Op or A or B)
    case (Op)
      ADD  :  Z = A + B;
      SUB  :  Z = A - B;
      MUL  :  Z = A * B;
      DIV  :  Z = A / B; // The A/B operation may not be
                         // supported by some synthesis tools.
    endcase
endmodule
// Synthesized netlist is shown in Figure 2-28.
```

A case statement behaves like a nested `if` statement, that is, the value of the case expression (*Op*) is checked with the first case item (*ADD*), if it does not match, the second case item (*SUB*) is checked and so on. The equivalent `if` statement for the above case statement is shown next.

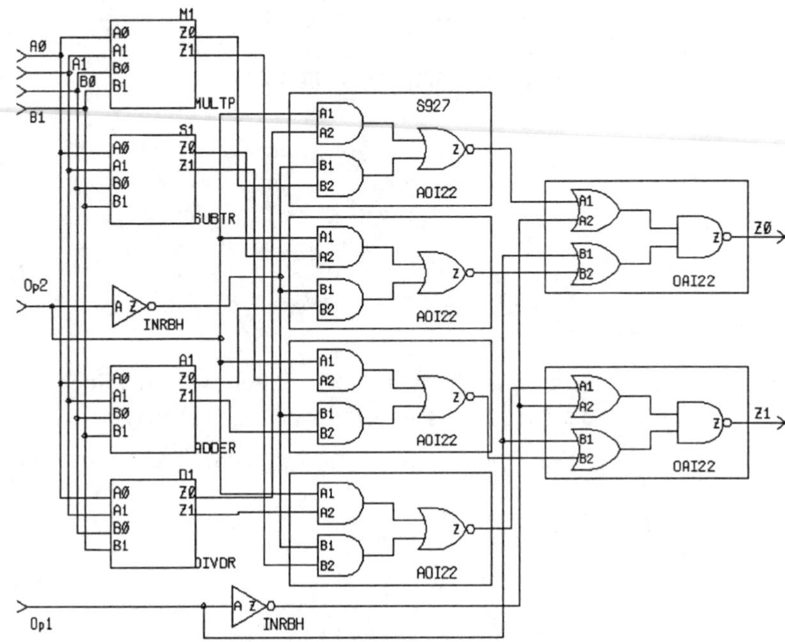

Figure 2-28 A 2-bit ALU.

```
if (Op == ADD)
  Z = A + B;
else if (Op == SUB)
  Z = A - B;
else if (Op == MUL)
  Z = A * B;
else if (Op == DIV)
  Z = A / B;
```

Here is another example of a case statement.

```
module CaseExample (DayOfWeek, SleepTime);
  input [1:3] DayOfWeek;
  output [1:4] SleepTime;
  reg [1:4] SleepTime;
  parameter MON = 0, TUE = 1, WED = 2, THU = 3, FRI = 4,
            SAT = 5, SUN = 6;
```

```
  always @ (DayOfWeek)
    case (DayOfWeek)
      MON,
      TUE,
      WED,
      THU:    SleepTime = 6;
      FRI:    SleepTime = 8;
      SAT:    SleepTime = 9;
      SUN:    SleepTime = 7;
      default: SleepTime = 10;       // Enjoy!
      // The default covers the case when DayOfWeek
      // has value 7.
    endcase
endmodule
// Synthesized netlist is shown in Figure 2-29.
```

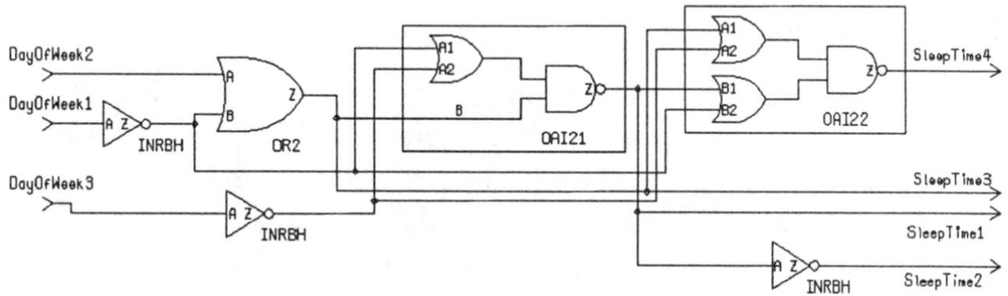

Figure 2-29 A case statement example.

Here is another example of a case statement.

```
module SelectAndAssign (CurrentState, RFlag);
  input [0:1] CurrentState;
  output [0:1] RFlag;
  reg [0:1] RFlag;

  parameter RESET = 2'b01, APPLY = 2'b11, WAITS = 2'b10,
          DONTCARE = 2'b00;

  always @ (CurrentState)
    case (CurrentState)
      RESET: RFlag = WAITS;
      APPLY: RFlag = RESET;
```

```
      WAITS: RFlag = APPLY;
      default : RFlag = DONTCARE;
    endcase
endmodule
// Synthesized netlist is shown in Figure 2-30.
```

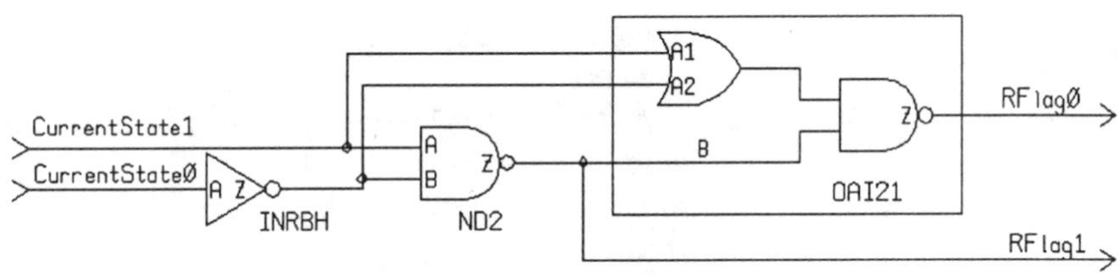

Figure 2-30 Logic generated from a case statement.

2.14.1 Casez Statement

In a casez statement, the value z is considered as a don't-care when it appears in a case item expression. The ? character can also be used alternatively for the character z. Values z and x are not allowed in a case expression. Additionally, value x cannot appear in a case item expression. Here is an example of a casez statement.

```
module CasezExample (ProgramCounter, DoCommand);
  input [0:3] ProgramCounter;
  output [0:1] DoCommand;
  reg [0:1] DoCommand;

  always @ (ProgramCounter)
    casez (ProgramCounter)
      4'b???1 : DoCommand = 0;
      4'b??10 : DoCommand = 1;
      4'b?100 : DoCommand = 2;
      4'b1000 : DoCommand = 3;
      default : DoCommand = 0;
    endcase
endmodule
// Synthesized netlist is shown in Figure 2-31.
```

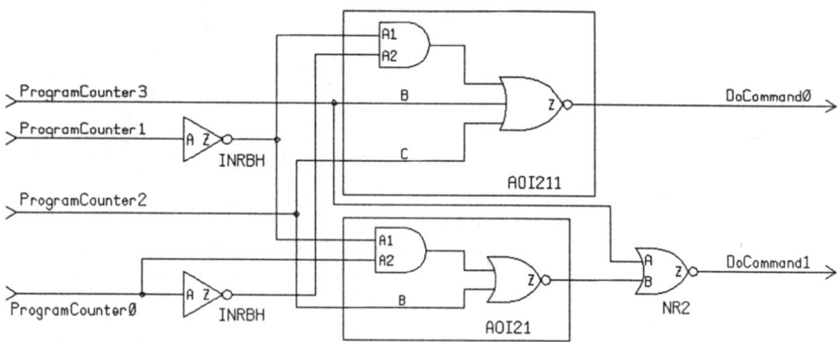

Figure 2-31 Casez statement example.

The casez statement is equivalent to the following `if` statement (note that the `?` character in a case item denotes a don't-care value).

```
if (ProgramCounter [3])
  DoCommand = 0;
else if (ProgramCounter [2:3] == 2'b10)
  DoCommand = 1;
else if (ProgramCounter [1:3] == 3'b100)
  DoCommand = 2;
else if (ProgramCounter [0:3] == 4'b1000)
  DoCommand = 3;
else
  DoCommand = 0;
```

2.14.2 Casex Statement

In a casex statement, the values x and z (? for a z is ok too) in a case item expression are considered as don't-care values. These values, for synthesis purposes, cannot appear as part of the case expression. Here is an example of a casex statement used to model a priority encoder.

```
module PriorityEncoder (Select, BitPosition);
  input [5:1] Select;
  output [2:0] BitPosition;
  reg [2:0] BitPosition;

  always @ (Select)
    casex (Select)
```

```
        5'bxxxx1 : BitPosition = 1;
        5'bxxx1x : BitPosition = 2;
        5'bxx1xx : BitPosition = 3;
        5'bx1xxx : BitPosition = 4;
        5'b1xxxx : BitPosition = 5;
        default : BitPosition = 0;
    endcase
endmodule
// Synthesized netlist is shown in Figure 2-32.
```

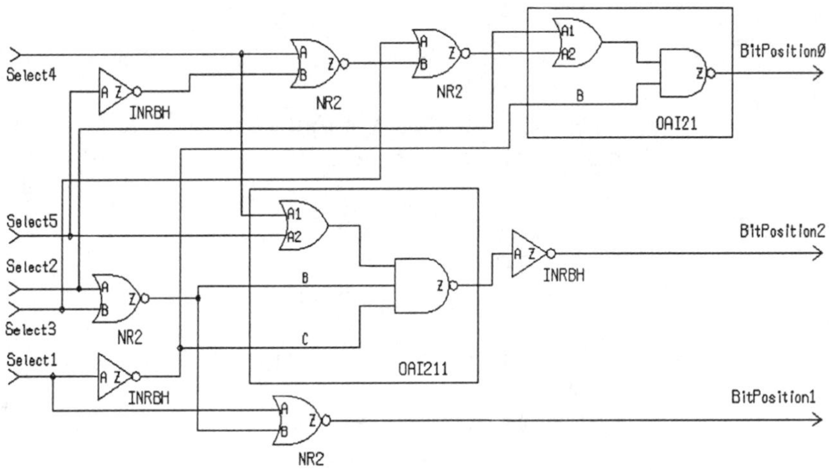

Figure 2-32 A priority encoder using casex statement.

The semantics of this casex statement can best be expressed by its equivalent `if` statement.

```
if (Select [1])
  BitPosition = 1;
else if (Select [2])
  BitPosition = 2;
else if (Select [3])
  BitPosition = 3;
else if (Select [4])
  BitPosition = 4;
else if (Select [5])
  BitPosition = 5;
```

```
else
  BitPosition = 0;
```

2.14.3 Inferring Latches from Case Statements

A latch may be inferred for a variable assigned in a case statement, just like in an `if` statement. If a variable is not assigned a value in all possible executions of the always statement, such as when a variable is assigned a value in only some branches of a case statement, a latch is inferred for that variable. See the following example.

```
module StateUpdate (CurrentState, Zip);
  input [0:1] CurrentState;
  output [0:1] Zip;
  reg [0:1] Zip;

  parameter S0 = 0, S1 = 1, S2 = 2, S3 = 3;

  always @ (CurrentState)
    case (CurrentState)
      S0,
      S3: Zip = 0;
      S1: Zip = 3;
    endcase
endmodule
// Synthesized netlist is shown in Figure 2-33.
```

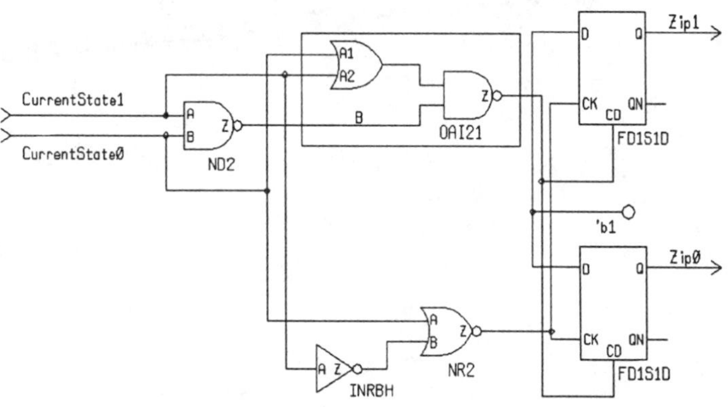

Figure 2-33 Latch inferred for a variable in a case statement.

The variable *Zip* is not assigned a value for all possible values of the input *CurrentState*. Therefore in keeping with the language semantics of a reg variable, a latch is inferred for *Zip*. The synthesized netlist shows the latch. In terms of latch inferencing, a case statement behaves identical to an `if` statement. If a latch is to be avoided, insert an initial value assignment to *Zip* before the case statement, as shown in the following code. The explicit assignment to *Zip* causes it to be defined for all values of *CurrentState*, and consequently for all possible executions of the always statement.

```
. . .
always @ (CurrentState)
begin
  Zip = 0;                    // This statement added.

  case (CurrentState)
  . . .
  endcase
end
```

The rules for inferring latches apply to casex and casez statements equally as well.

2.14.4 Full Case

In the previous section, we saw that a latch may be inferred for a variable that is not assigned a value for all possible values of a case expression. Sometimes it is the case that the designer does not expect the case expression to have any value other than those listed in the case items. Here is an example.

```
module NextStateLogic (NextToggle, Toggle);
  input [1:0] Toggle;
  output [1:0] NextToggle;
  reg [1:0] NextToggle;

  always @ (Toggle)
    case (Toggle)
      2'b01 : NextToggle = 2'b10;
      2'b10 : NextToggle = 2'b01;
    endcase
```

```
endmodule
// Synthesized netlist is shown in Figure 2-34.
```

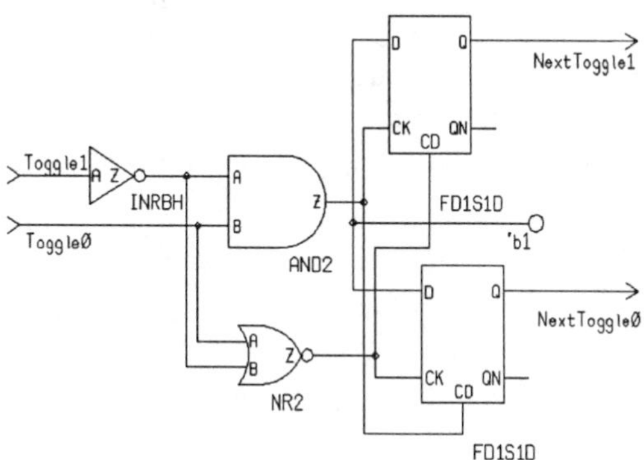

Figure 2-34 Latches are inferred for *NextToggle*.

The designer knows that *Toggle* cannot have any value other than 2'b01 and 2'b10. This information needs to be passed to the synthesis tool. If such information is not provided to the synthesis tool, latches are inferred for *NextToggle* (the two FD1S1D's in Figure 2-34) since it is not assigned a value for the case expression values 2'b00 and 2'b11. Such information is passed to a synthesis tool via a synthesis directive called *full_case*. A *synthesis directive* is a special code in the model that provides additional information to a synthesis tool. The full_case synthesis directive is specified as a Verilog HDL comment in the model associated with the case statement; since the synthesis directive appears as a comment, it has no effect on the language semantics of the model.

A synthesis tool on encountering such a directive on a case statement understands that all possible values (that can occur in the design) of the case expression have been listed and no other values are possible. Consequently, a variable assigned in all branches of the case statement will never infer a latch. Here is the case statement in the *NextStateLogic* module with the directive specified.

```
module NextStateLogicFullCase (NextToggle, Toggle);
  input [1:0] Toggle;
  output [1:0] NextToggle;
  reg [1:0] NextToggle;
```

```
    always @ (Toggle)
      case (Toggle)              // synthesis full_case
        2'b01 : NextToggle = 2'b10;
        2'b10 : NextToggle = 2'b01;
      endcase
  endmodule
  // Synthesized netlist is shown in Figure 2-35.
```

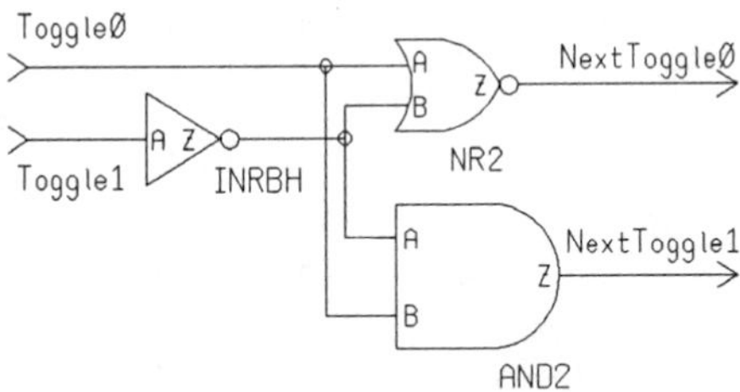

Figure 2-35 With full_case synthesis directive: no latches.

As the synthesized netlist shows, no latches are inferred for *NextToggle* when the full_case synthesis directive is used.

An alternative way to avoid latches in the above example is to specify a default branch in the case statement or to make a default assignment to all variables assigned in a case statement (in this example, *NextToggle*), prior to the case statement. Here is an example that uses a default branch to avoid inferring latches.

```
always @ (Toggle)
  case (Toggle)
    2'b01 : NextToggle = 2'b10;
    2'b10 : NextToggle = 2'b01;
    default : NextToggle = 2'b01; // Dummy assignment.
  endcase
```

Here is the always statement that has a default assignment for *NextToggle*; no latches are inferred for *NextToggle*.

```
always @ (Toggle)
begin
```

```
    NextToggle = 2'b01;              // Default assignment.

    case (Toggle)
      2'b01 : NextToggle = 2'b10;
      2'b10 : NextToggle = 2'b01;
    endcase
  end
```

Caution, use of the full_case directive can potentially lead to a functional mismatch between the design model and the synthesized netlist; see Chapter 5 for such examples.

2.14.5 Parallel Case

Verilog HDL semantics of a case statement specifies a priority order in which a case branch is selected. The case expression is checked with the first case item, if it is not the same, the next case item is checked, if not the same, the next case item is checked, and so on. A priority order of case item checking is implied by the case statement. Additionally, in Verilog HDL, it is possible for two or more case item values to be the same or there may be overlapping case item values such as in casex and casez statements; however, because of the priority order, only the first one in the listed sequence of case items is selected.

To apply the strict semantics of a case statement in synthesis to hardware, a nested if-like structure (priority logic: if this do this, else if this do this, else . . .) is synthesized. Here is an example of a case statement.

```
module PriorityLogic (NextToggle, Toggle);
  input [2:0] Toggle;
  output [2:0] NextToggle;
  reg [2:0] NextToggle;

  always @ (Toggle)
    casex (Toggle)
      3'bxx1 : NextToggle = 3'b010;
      3'bx1x : NextToggle = 3'b110;
      3'b1xx : NextToggle = 3'b001;
      default : NextToggle = 3'b000;
    endcase
endmodule
// Synthesized netlist is shown in Figure 2-36.
```

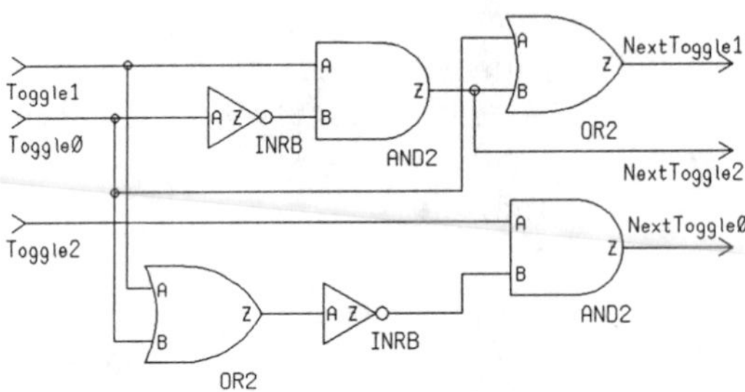

Figure 2-36 Priority logic selects each branch.

The equivalent behavior of the case statement is expressed in the following `if` statement.

```
if (Toggle[0] == 'b1)
  NextToggle = 3'b010;
else if (Toggle[1] == 'b1)
  NextToggle = 3'b110;
else if (Toggle[2] == 'b1)
  NextToggle = 3'b001;
else
  NextToggle = 3'b000;
```

What if the designer knows that all case item values are mutually exclusive? In such a case, a decoder can be synthesized for a case statement control (the case expression is checked for all possible values of the case item values in parallel) instead of the priority logic (which could potentially be nested deep depending on the number of branches in the case statement).

The information that all case item values are mutually exclusive needs to be passed to the synthesis tool. This is done by using a synthesis directive called *parallel_case*. When such a directive is attached to a case statement, a synthesis tool interprets the case statement as if all case items are mutually exclusive. Since the synthesis directive appears as a comment in the Verilog HDL model, it has no effect on the language semantics of the model. This implies that no priority logic is synthesized for the case statement control; instead decoding logic is used. Here is the case statement with the parallel_case directive.

```
module ParallelCase (NextToggle, Toggle);
  input [2:0] Toggle;
  output [2:0] NextToggle;
  reg [2:0] NextToggle;

  always @ (Toggle)
    casex (Toggle)            // synthesis parallel_case
      3'bxx1 : NextToggle = 3'b010;
      3'bx1x : NextToggle = 3'b110;
      3'b1xx : NextToggle = 3'b001;
      default : NextToggle = 3'b000;
    endcase
endmodule
// Synthesized netlist is shown in Figure 2-37.
```

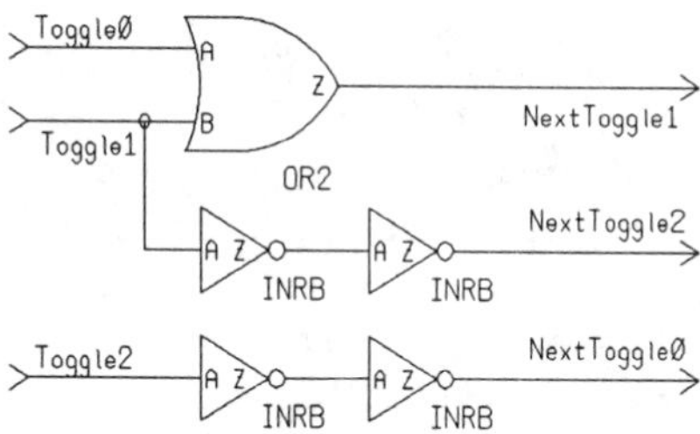

Figure 2-37 With parallel_case directive: no priority logic.

The equivalent synthesis interpretation for the case statement is as follows (with only one `if` condition guaranteed to be true).

```
if (Toggle[0] == 'b1)
  NextToggle = 3'b010;

if (Toggle[1] == 'b1)
  NextToggle = 3'b110;

if (Toggle[2] == 'b1)
  NextToggle = 3'b001;

if ((Toggle[0] != 'b1) &&
     (Toggle[1] != 'b1) &&
```

```
      (Toggle[2] != 'b1))
    NextToggle = 3'b000;
```

With the synthesis directive, decoding logic is synthesized for the branching logic as shown in Figure 2-37. Without the synthesis directive, priority logic is synthesized as shown in Figure 2-36.

A word of caution. The synthesis directive, parallel_case, can potentially cause a functional mismatch between the design model and the synthesized netlist; Chapter 5 elaborates on this further.

2.14.6 Non-constant as Case Item

In Verilog HDL, it is possible to have a non-constant expression as a case item. This is shown in the following example of a priority encoder.

```
module PriorityEncoder (Pbus, Address);
  input [0:3] Pbus;
  output [0:1] Address;
  reg [0:1] Address;

  always @ (Pbus)
    case (1'b1)                  // synthesis full_case
      Pbus[0] : Address = 2'b00;
      Pbus[1] : Address = 2'b01;
      Pbus[2] : Address = 2'b10;
      Pbus[3] : Address = 2'b11;
    endcase
endmodule
// Synthesized netlist is shown in Figure 2-38.
```

It is necessary to specify the full_case synthesis directive, otherwise latches are inferred for *Address*. Alternatively, an initial assignment to *Address* before the case statement can also be made to avoid latches; no synthesis directive is then necessary. This is shown in the following always statement.

```
  always @ (Pbus)
  begin
    Address = 2'b00;
```

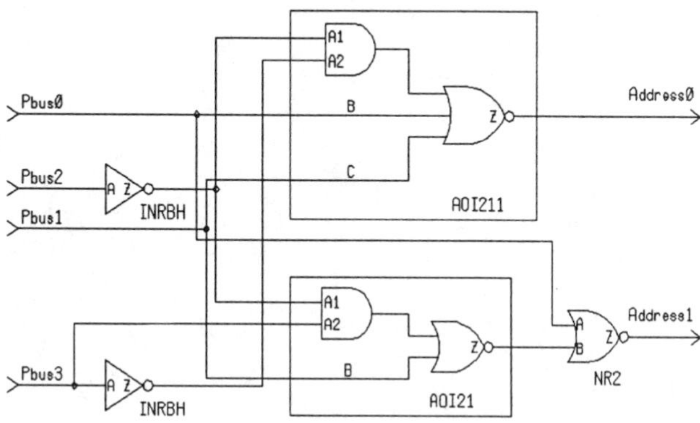

Figure 2-38 Priority encoder using case statement.

```
    case (1'b1)
      Pbus[0] : Address = 2'b00;
      Pbus[1] : Address = 2'b01;
      Pbus[2] : Address = 2'b10;
      Pbus[3] : Address = 2'b11;
    endcase
  end
```

2.15 More on Inferring Latches

A latch can be inferred by using an incompletely specified `if` statement or a case statement, that is, if a variable is not assigned a value in all branches of an `if` statement or a case statement, a latch is inferred for that variable. Here is an example.

```
module LatchExample (ClockA, CurrentState, NextState);
  input ClockA;
  input [3:0] CurrentState;
  output [3:0] NextState;
  reg [3:0] NextState;

  always @ (ClockA or CurrentState)
    if (ClockA)
      NextState = CurrentState;
```

```
endmodule
// Synthesized netlist is shown in Figure 2-39.
```

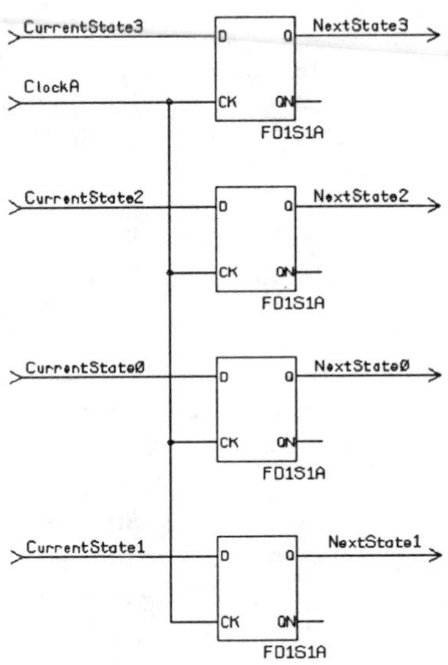

Figure 2-39 An incompletely specified condition infers a latch.

The variable *NextState* is assigned a value only when *ClockA* is 1. If *ClockA* is 0, *NextState* retains its previous value, thus inferring a latch.

Locally Declared Variable

A variable declared locally within an always statement is also inferred as a latch if it is incompletely assigned in a conditional statement (`if` statement or case statement). This is shown in the following module.

```
module LocalIntLatch (Clock, CurrentState, NextState);
  input Clock;
  input [3:0] CurrentState;
  output [3:0] NextState;
  reg [3:0] NextState;

  always @ (Clock or CurrentState)
  begin: L1
    integer Temp;
```

```
    if (Clock)
      Temp = CurrentState;

    NextState = Temp;
  end
endmodule
// Synthesized netlist is shown in Figure 2-40.
```

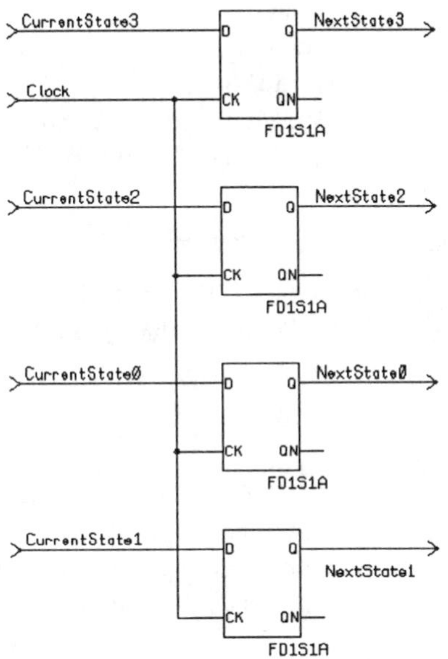

Figure 2-40 A local integer can also be a latch.

Variable Assigned Before Use

If a variable is assigned and used within a conditional branch, no latch is necessary as shown in the following module. This is because the value of variable *Temp* need not be saved between level changes of *Clock*.

```
module LocalIntNoLatch (Clock, CurrentState,
                        NextState);
  input Clock;
  input [3:0] CurrentState;
  output [3:0] NextState;
```

```
  reg [3:0] NextState;

  always @ (Clock or CurrentState)
  begin: L1
    integer Temp;

    if (Clock)
    begin
      Temp = CurrentState;
      NextState = Temp;
    end
  end
endmodule
// Synthesized netlist is same as one
// shown in Figure 2-40.
```

Use Before Assigned

If a variable is used before it is assigned in an incompletely specified conditional statement, then a latch is inferred. Here is such a module.

```
module RegUsedBeforeDef (ClockZ, CurrentState,
                         NextState);
  input ClockZ;
  input [3:0] CurrentState;
  output [3:0] NextState;
  reg [3:0] NextState;

  reg [3:0] Temp;

  always @ (ClockZ or CurrentState or Temp)
    if (ClockZ)
    begin
      NextState = Temp;
      Temp = CurrentState;
    end
endmodule
// Synthesized netlist is shown in Figure 2-41.
```

What about if *Temp* is an integer?

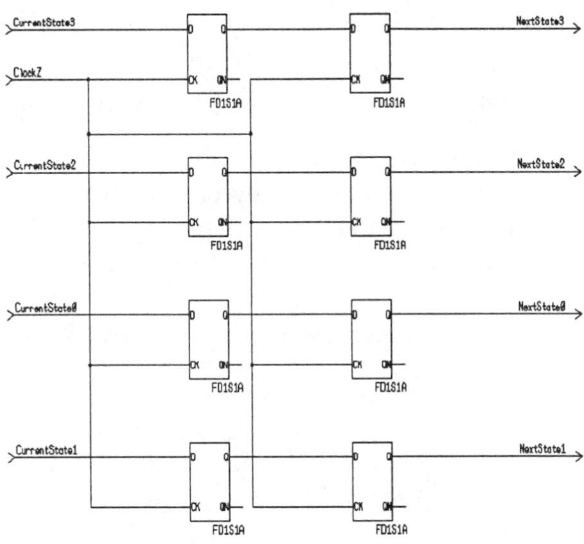

Figure 2-41 A variable used before being assigned in a conditional.

```
module LocalIntUsedBeforeDef (ClockY, CurrentState,
                              NextState);
  input ClockY;
  input [3:0] CurrentState;
  output [3:0] NextState;
  reg [3:0] NextState;

  always @ (ClockY or CurrentState)
  begin: L1
    integer LocalInt;

    if (ClockY)
    begin
      NextState = LocalInt;
      LocalInt = CurrentState;
    end
  end
endmodule
```

A synthesis system may produce an error in such a case indicating that the local integer *LocalInt* is used before its definition. Alternately a synthesis system may produce a warning and not generate any latches for the local integer.

2.15.1 Latch with Asynchronous Preset and Clear

If a variable, that is inferred as a latch, is assigned constant values in some branches of a conditional statement, bits that are 1 get assigned to the preset terminal of the latch, while those with 0 get assigned to the clear terminal. This is shown in the following example.

```
module AsyncLatch (ClockX, Reset, Set, CurrentState,
                   NextState);
  input ClockX, Reset, Set;
  input [3:0] CurrentState;
  output [3:0] NextState;
  reg [3:0] NextState;

  always @ (Reset or Set or ClockX or CurrentState)
    if (! Reset)
      NextState = 12;
    else if (! Set)
      NextState = 5;
    else if (! ClockX)
      NextState = CurrentState;
endmodule
// Synthesized netlist is shown in Figure 2-42.
```

Four latches, with preset and clear terminals as appropriately required, are synthesized for *NextState*.

For the above example, a synthesis tool may alternately not generate a latch with asynchronous preset and clear, but direct the preset clear logic into the D-input of a simple latch. This is shown in the synthesized netlist that appears in Figure 2-43.

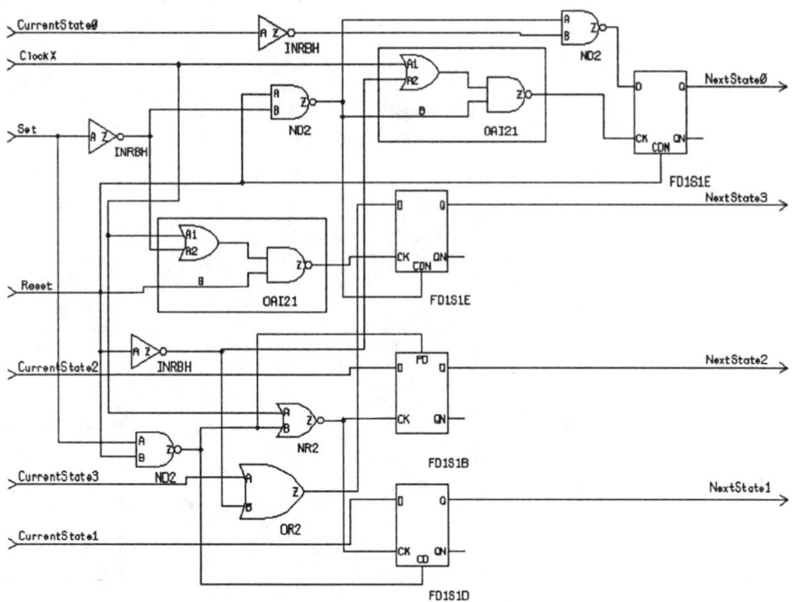

Figure 2-42 Latch with asynchronous preset and clear.

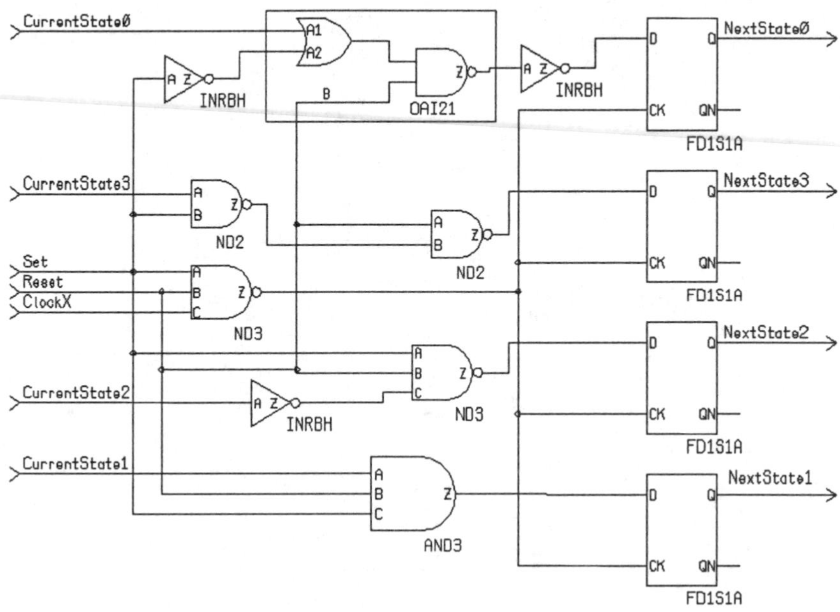

Figure 2-43 Latches with no asynchronous preset and clear.

2.16 Loop Statement

There are four kinds of loop statements in Verilog HDL.

- while-loop
- for-loop
- forever-loop
- repeat-loop

The for-loop statement is the one typically supported for synthesis. A for-loop is implemented by unrolling the for-loop, that is, all statements within the for-loop are replicated, once for each value of the for-loop index. This puts a restriction on the for-loop bounds, which must therefore evaluate to constants. Here is an example of a for-loop statement.

```
module DeMultiplexer (Address, Line);
  input [1:0] Address;
```

```
  output [3:0] Line;
  reg [3:0] Line;

  integer J;

  always @ (Address)
    for (J = 3; J >= 0; J = J - 1)
      if (Address == J)
        Line[J] = 1;
      else
        Line[J] = 0;
endmodule
// Synthesized netlist is shown in Figure 2-44.
```

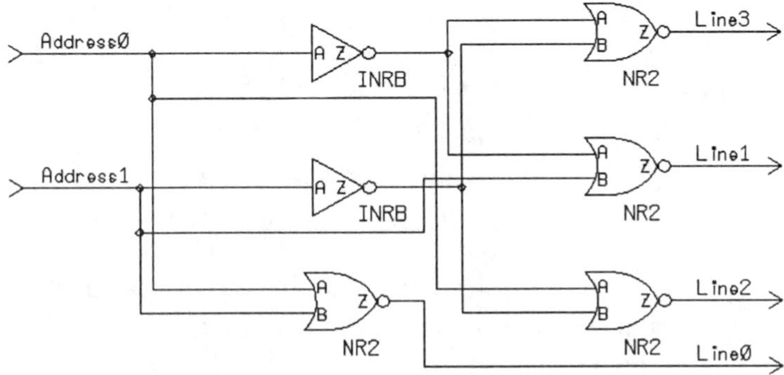

Figure 2-44 A for-loop example.

When the for-loop is expanded, the following four `if` statements are obtained.

```
if (Address == 3) Line[3] = 1; else Line[3] = 0;
if (Address == 2) Line[2] = 1; else Line[2] = 0;
if (Address == 1) Line[1] = 1; else Line[1] = 0;
if (Address == 0) Line[0] = 1; else Line[0] = 0;
```

2.17 Modeling Flip-flops

A flip-flop is inferred from a variable when it is assigned a value in a special form of always statement. This always statement is of the form:

```
always @ (<clock_event>)
  <statement>
```

where *<clock_event>* is one of:

```
posedge <clock_name>
negedge <clock_name>
```

The semantics of the always statement implies that all statements in *<statement>* are to be executed only when a rising edge or a falling edge of clock occurs. We shall call this special always statement as a *clocked always statement*.

When modeling sequential logic, it is recommended that a non-blocking procedural assignment be used for a variable that is assigned in a clocked always statement and its value used outside of the always statement; this is to prevent any possibility of functional mismatch between the design model and its synthesized netlist. Such a target of a non-blocking assignment that appears in a clocked always statement accurately models the behavior of a sequential element.

Here is a simple example.

```
module PickOne (A, B, Clock, Control, Zee);
  input A, B, Clock, Control;
  output Zee;
  reg Zee;

  always @ (negedge Clock)
    if (Control)
      Zee <= A;
    else
      Zee <= B;
endmodule
// Synthesized netlist is shown in Figure 2-45.
```

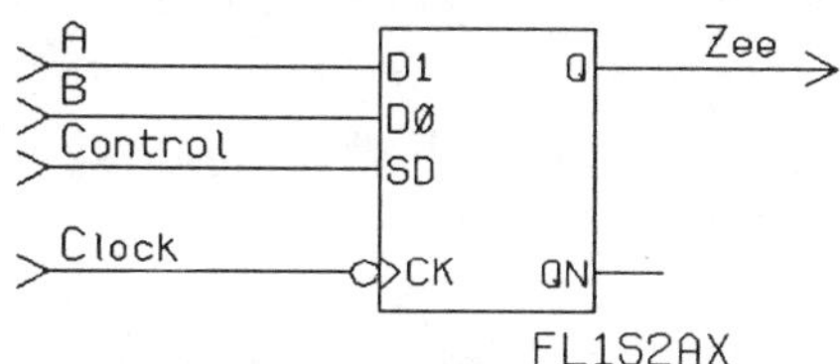

Figure 2-45 Sequential logic synthesized using a special always statement.

The assignment to output *Zee* occurs only at the falling edge of the clock. Variable *Zee* is inferred to be a falling-edge-triggered flip-flop. The flip-flop shown in the figure has a data-select, that is, the input *Control* selects either *A* or *B* as the data for the flip-flop.

Here is another example.

```
module Incrementor (ClockA, Counter);
  parameter COUNTER_SIZE = 2;
  input ClockA;
  output [COUNTER_SIZE-1:0] Counter;
  reg [COUNTER_SIZE-1:0] Counter;

  always @ (posedge ClockA)
    Counter <= Counter + 1;
endmodule
// Synthesized netlist is shown in Figure 2-46.
```

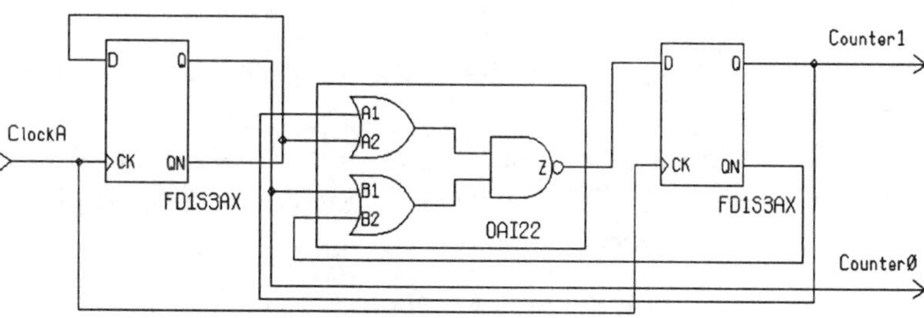

Figure 2-46 Modeling flip-flops.

The logic in the always statement implies that every time there is a rising edge on *ClockA*, variable *Counter* is incremented. Since *Counter* is assigned under the control of a clock edge, rising-edge-triggered flip-flops are synthesized for *Counter*.

Here is a model of an up-down counter that shows flip-flops being modeled.

```
module UpDownCounter (Control, ClockB, Counter);
  input Control, ClockB;
  output [1:0] Counter;
  reg [1:0] Counter;

  always @ (negedge ClockB)
    if (Control)
      Counter <= Counter + 1;
    else
      Counter <= Counter - 1;
endmodule
// Synthesized netlist is shown in Figure 2-47.
```

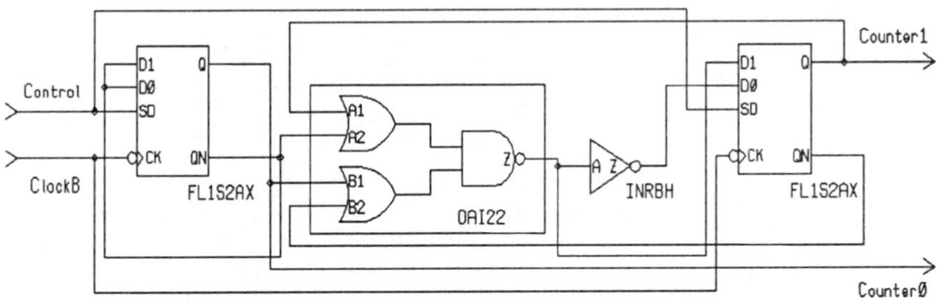

Figure 2-47 Falling-edge-triggered flip-flops inferred.

The variable *Counter* is assigned under the control of a falling edge of clock *ClockB*. Thus, two falling-edge-triggered flip-flops are synthesized for *Counter*.

Flip-flop inference rule is simple: If a variable is assigned a value under the control of a clock edge, a flip-flop is generated; an exception to this rule is when a variable is assigned and used only locally within an always statement as an intermediate variable.

Here is another example.

```
module FlipFlop (Clk, CurrentState, NextState);
  input Clk;
  input [3:0] CurrentState;
  output [3:0] NextState;
  reg [3:0] NextState;

  always @(posedge Clk)
    NextState <= CurrentState;
endmodule
// Synthesized netlist is shown in Figure 2-48.
```

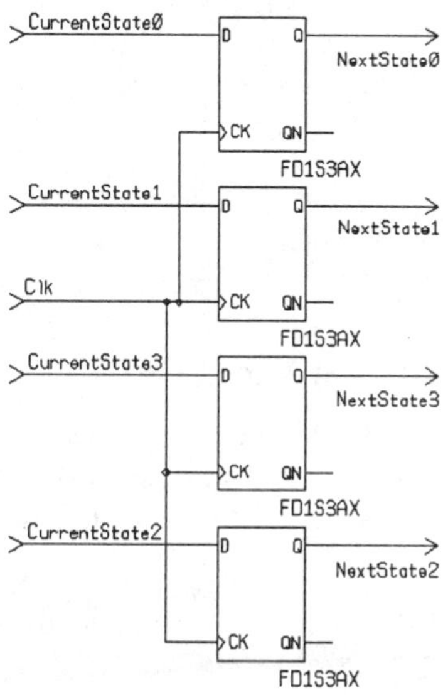

Figure 2-48 Flip-flops inferred from a variable assigned under clock control.

In this example, *NextState* is assigned a value only if there is a rising edge on *Clk*. Thus, four rising-edge-triggered flip-flops (needed to store values 0 through 15) are inferred for reg *NextState*.

If a falling-edge-triggered flip-flop are to be inferred, then the clock edge event "**posedge** *Clk*" needs to be replaced by:

```
negedge Clk
```

Integer variables assigned under the control of a clock edge are also inferred as flip-flops. Here is an example where an integer variable is assigned under clock control. Four flip-flops are inferred for the variable *IntState*; the other high-order bits of the variable are optimized away (since they are not used).

```
module FlipFlopInt (Clk, CurrentState, NextState);
  input Clk;
  input [3:0] CurrentState;
  output [3:0] NextState;

  integer IntState;

  always @(posedge Clk)
    IntState <= CurrentState;

  assign NextState = IntState;
endmodule
// Synthesized netlist is same as Figure 2-48.
```

Local Use of Variables

In all the above cases, a variable was assigned under the control of a clock and its value was used outside of the always statement, thus requiring its value to be saved in a flip-flop.

What if a variable is defined globally (outside the always statement) but used only locally within an always statement? Here is an example.

```
module GlobalReg (Clk, CurrentState, NextState);
  input Clk;
  input [3:0] CurrentState;
  output [3:0] NextState;
  reg [3:0] NextState;

  reg [3:0] Temp;

  always @(negedge Clk)
  begin
    Temp = CurrentState;
    NextState <= Temp;
  end
endmodule
```

Even though *Temp* is assigned under the control of the clock, no flip-flops are inferred for *Temp* since it is assigned a value first and then used, all within the same clock cycle. The synthesized netlist is same as Figure 2-48. In this case, *Temp* is merely being used as a temporary (as an intermediate variable), and therefore a blocking assignment should be used to reflect the fact that the use of *Temp* in the second statement is the value of *Temp* assigned in the first statement. A non-blocking assignment is used for the *NextState* assignment as *NextState* infers flip-flops.

What happens in the above case if we switch the order of the statements around? In this case, since the value of *Temp* is used before its assignment, its value needs to be retained across multiple clock cycles, thereby inferring flip-flops for *Temp*. *Temp* models the internal state of the always statement. This is shown in the following example, where *Temp* is used before its assignment.

```
module RegUseDef (Clk, CurrentState, NextState);
  input Clk;
  input [3:0] CurrentState;
  output [3:0] NextState;
  reg [3:0] NextState;

  reg [3:0] Temp;

  always @(negedge Clk)
  begin
    NextState <= Temp;
    Temp = CurrentState;
  end
endmodule
// Synthesized netlist is shown in Figure 2-49.
```

In this case, falling-edge-triggered flip-flops are inferred for variable *Temp*, in addition to those for *NextState*.

What if variables are declared locally within an always statement?

Variables (reg and integer types) declared locally within an always statement do not infer flip-flops. This may potentially lead to a functional mismatch between the Verilog HDL model and the synthesized netlist. Here is an example of a locally declared variable *Temp* that does not get inferred as a flip-flop.

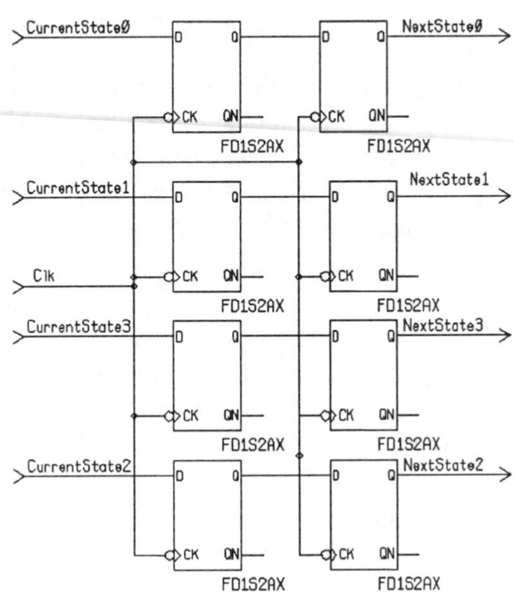

Figure 2-49 A variable used before its definition is inferred as a flip-flop.

```
module LocalVarAssignUse (Clk, CurrentState,
                          NextState);
  input Clk;
  input [3:0] CurrentState;
  output [3:0] NextState;
  reg [3:0] NextState;

  always @(posedge Clk)
  begin: LabelA
    reg [3:0] Temp;

    Temp = CurrentState;
    NextState <= Temp;
  end
endmodule
```

No flip-flops are inferred for *Temp* since it is locally declared within the always statement and a value is assigned to the variable and used immediately in the same clock edge. Flip-flops are inferred for *NextState* (as this is used outside the always statement). The synthesized netlist is same as the one shown in Figure 2-48.

However, a potential for mismatch exists between the design model and its synthesized netlist if the order of the above statements are reversed. This is because no flip-flops are inferred for locally declared variables. Here is such a model.

```
module LocalVarUseAssign (Clk, CurrentState,
                          NextState);
  input Clk;
  input [3:0] CurrentState;
  output [3:0] NextState;
  reg [3:0] NextState;

  always @(posedge Clk)
  begin: LabelA
    reg [3:0] Temp;

    NextState <= Temp;
    Temp = CurrentState;
  end
endmodule
```

The synthesized netlist is the same as in Figure 2-48. Notice that on every clock edge, *NextState* always get the value of *Temp* assigned in the previous clock cycle, but not so in the synthesized netlist. The recommendation here is to avoid using locally declared variables in this fashion. Hopefully a synthesis tool will issue a warning if no flip-flops are inferred for *Temp*.

2.17.1 Multiple Clocks

It is possible to have a single module that has multiple clocked always statements. Here is such an example of multiple clocks used in a single model.

```
module MultipleClocks (Vt15Clock, AddClock, AdN,
      ResetN, SubClr, SubN, Ds1Clock, Ds1Add, Ds1Sub);
  input Vt15Clock, AddClock, AdN, ResetN, SubClr,
      SubN, Ds1Clock;
  output Ds1Add, Ds1Sub;
  reg Ds1Add, Ds1Sub;
```

```
  reg AddState, SubState;

  always @ (posedge Vt15Clock)
  begin
    AddState <= AddClock ^~ (AdN | ResetN);
    SubState <= SubClr ^ (SubN & ResetN);
  end

  always @ (posedge Ds1Clock)
  begin
    Ds1Add <= AddState;
    Ds1Sub <= SubState;
  end
endmodule
// Synthesized netlist is shown in Figure 2-50.
```

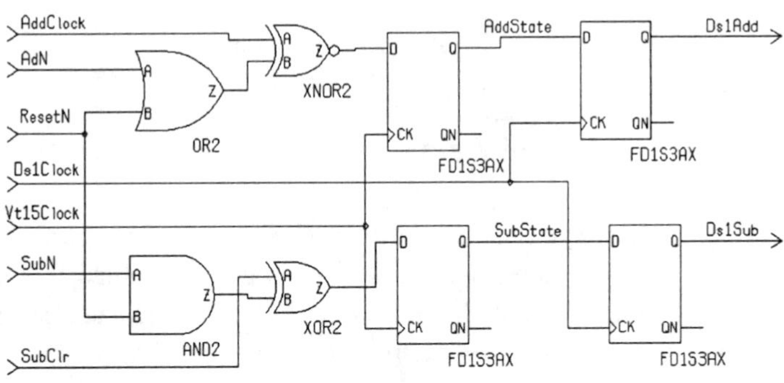

Figure 2-50 Multiple clocks within an always statement.

This module has two always statements. The statements in the first always statement are controlled by a positive edge of clock *Vt15Clock*, while the statements in the second always statement are controlled by the positive edge of clock *Ds1Clock*.

A restriction usually imposed by a synthesis system is that a variable cannot be assigned under the control of more than one clock. For example, it would be illegal to assign to *AddState* in the second always statement.

2.17.2 Multi-phase Clocks

It is possible to have a single module with multiple clocked always statements in which different edges of the same clock are used. Here is such an example in which two different phases of the same clock are used.

```
module MultiPhaseClocks (Clk, A, B, C, E);
  input Clk, A, B, C;
  output E;
  reg E, D;

  always @ (posedge Clk)
    E <= D | C;

  always @ (negedge Clk)
    D <= A & B;
endmodule
// Synthesized netlist is shown in Figure 2-51.
```

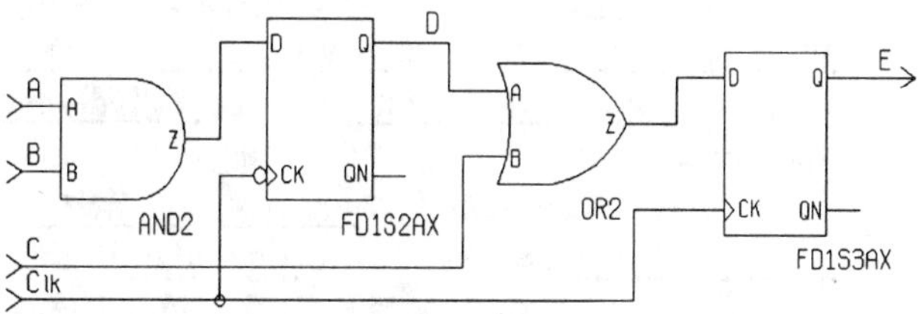

Figure 2-51 Different edges of the same clock within a single module.

In this module, the statements in the first always statement are controlled by the positive edge of *Clk*, while the statements in the second always statement are controlled by the negative edge of *Clk*.

A restriction usually imposed by a synthesis system in this case is that a variable cannot be assigned under two different clock conditions or for that matter, under different clock edges. For example, it would be illegal to assign a value to *D* in the first always statement.

2.17.3 With Asynchronous Preset and Clear

So far we have talked about synthesizing simple D-type flip-flops. What if we wanted to infer a flip-flop with asynchronous preset and clear? To generate such a flip-flop, a special form of `if` statement has to be used. This is best shown with an example template.

```
always @ (posedge A or negedge B or negedge C . . .
        or posedge Clock)
  if (A)                    // posedge A.
    <statement>             // Asynchronous logic.
  else if ( ! B)            // negedge B.
    <statement>             // Asynchronous logic.
  else if ( ! C)            // negedge C.
    <statement>             // Asynchronous logic.
  . . .                     // Any number of else if's.
  else                      // posedge Clock implied.
    <statement>             // Synchronous logic.
```

The event list (the parenthesized list following the @ symbol) in the always statement can have any number of edge events, either **posedge** or **negedge**. One of the events must be a clock event. The remaining events specify conditions under which asynchronous logic are to be executed. The always statement has exactly one `if` statement with many `else if`'s. Each `if` corresponds to one edge in the event list. The last `else` implicitly corresponds to the clock edge. The conditions for the `if` statements must match the edge type specified in the event list. For example, if "**posedge** *A*" is present in the event list, then the `if` statement starts of as:

```
if (A)
```

If "**negedge** *B*" is present in event list, then the `if` statement starts of as:

```
if (! B )
```

The statements within each `if` branch (except the last) represents asynchronous logic, while the statement in the last `else` branch represents synchronous logic.

If a variable is assigned a value in any of the asynchronous sections and is also assigned in the synchronous part, that variable will get synthesized as a flip-flop with asynchronous preset and or clear. Depending on the value being assigned, the flip-flop could either be a flip-flop with asynchronous preset (if a non-zero value is assigned), or a flip-flop with asynchronous clear (if a zero value is being assigned), or a flip-flop with both.

Here is an example of an up-down counter with asynchronous preset and clear.

```
module AsyncPreClrCounter (Clock, Preset, UpDown,
                          Clear, PresetData, Counter);
  parameter NUM_BITS = 2;
  input Clock, Preset, UpDown, Clear;
  input [NUM_BITS-1:0] PresetData;
  output [NUM_BITS-1:0] Counter;
  reg [NUM_BITS-1:0] Counter;

  always @ (posedge Preset or posedge Clear or
            posedge Clock)
    if (Preset)
      Counter <= PresetData;
    else if (Clear)
      Counter <= 0;
    else                    // Implicit posedge Clock.
    begin                   // Synchronous part.
      if (UpDown)
        Counter <= Counter + 1;
      else
        Counter <= Counter - 1;
    end
endmodule
// Synthesized netlist is shown in Figure 2-52.
```

Having an asynchronous data input such as *PresetData* can cause a problem. Consider when *Preset* is 1 and then *PresetData* changes. The change of *PresetData* does not reflect in the Verilog HDL model while the change propagates to *Counter* in the synthesized netlist. Avoid or be careful when using asynchronous data inputs.

Here is another example of inferring a flip-flop with asynchronous preset and clear.

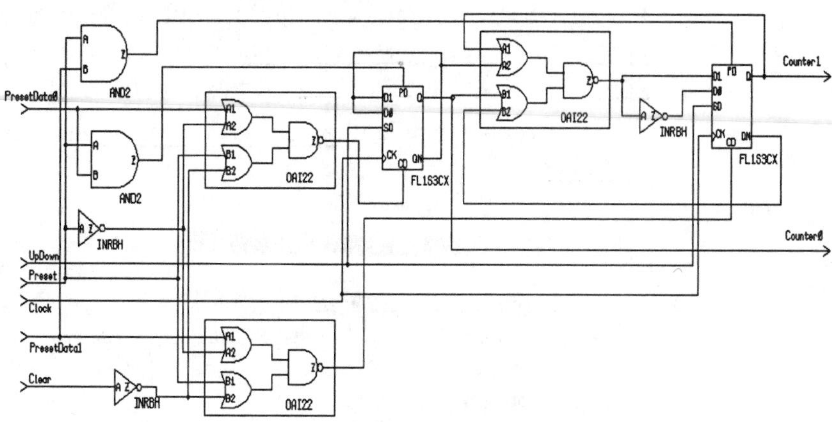

Figure 2-52 Flip-flops with asynchronous preset and clear.

```
module AsyncFlipFlop (ClkA, Reset, Set, CurrentState,
                       NextState);
  input ClkA, Reset, Set;
  input [3:0] CurrentState;
  output [3:0] NextState;
  reg [3:0] NextState;

  always @ (negedge Reset or negedge Set or negedge ClkA)
    if (! Reset)
      NextState <= 12;                  // Stmt A.
    else if (! Set)
      NextState <= 5;                   // Stmt B.
    else
      NextState <= CurrentState;        // Stmt C.
endmodule
// Synthesized netlist is shown in Figure 2-53.
```

Since *NextState* is assigned a value under the control of a clock edge (Stmt *C*) and it is also assigned asynchronously (Stmt *A* and *B*), a falling-edge-triggered flip-flop with asynchronous preset and clear is synthesized. This is shown in Figure 2-53. Note that four flip-flops are required. The first flip-flop (the leftmost bit of *NextState*) has both asynchronous preset and clear terminals since it needs to be preset on *Reset* and cleared on *Set*. Similarly, the fourth flip-flop has both asynchronous preset and clear terminals since it needs to be preset on *Set* and cleared on *Reset*. The

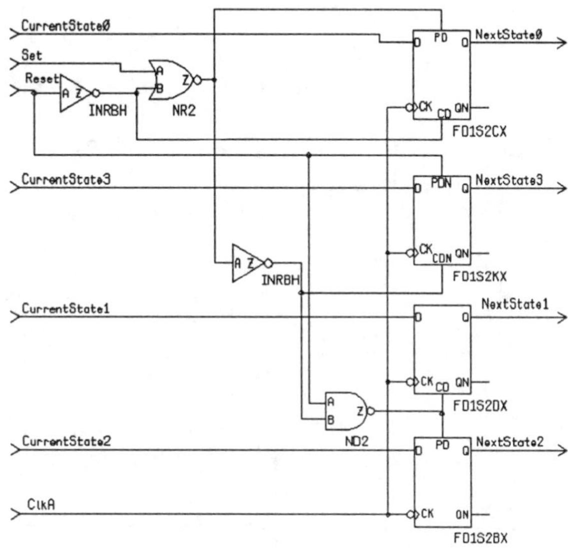

Figure 2-53 Flip-flops with asynchronous preset and clear.

second flip-flop has only a preset terminal since a 'b1 is asynchronously assigned in both the conditions, while the third flip-flop has only a clear terminal since a 'b0 is assigned under both the conditions.

2.17.4 With Synchronous Preset and Clear

What if we want to model a flip-flop with synchronous preset and clear? In such a case, simply describe the synchronous preset and clear logic within a clocked always statement (an always statement with a clock event). Here is an example.

```
module SyncPresetCounter (Clock, Preset, UpDown,
                          PresetData, Counter);
  parameter NBITS = 2;
  input Clock, Preset, UpDown;
  input [0:NBITS-1] PresetData;
  output [0:NBITS-1] Counter;
  reg [0:NBITS-1] Counter;

  always @ (negedge Clock)
    if (Preset)
```

```
        Counter <= PresetData;
    else
      if (UpDown)
        Counter <= Counter + 1;
      else
        Counter <= Counter - 1;
endmodule
// Synthesized netlist is shown in Figure 2-54.
```

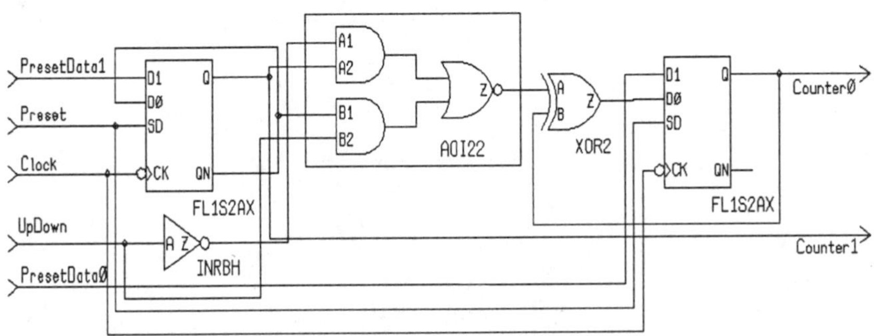

Figure 2-54 Synchronous preset clear synthesized as combinational logic.

There are two approaches to synthesize this model. One approach is to direct the *PresetData* input into the synchronous preset input of the synthesized flip-flops; alternatively, the *PresetData* could be directed directly into the data input of the flip-flops. The synthesized netlist shown here shows the latter option; a synthesis system may optionally synthesize to the alternate approach.

Let us look at another example.

```
module SyncFlipFlop (ClkB, Reset, Set, CurrentState,
                    NextState);
  input ClkB, Reset, Set;
  input [3:0] CurrentState;
  output [3:0] NextState;
  reg [3:0] NextState;

  always @ (negedge ClkB)
    if (! Reset)
      NextState <= 12;
```

```
    else if (! Set)
      NextState <= 5;
    else
      NextState <= CurrentState;
endmodule
// Synthesized netlist is shown in Figure 2-55.
```

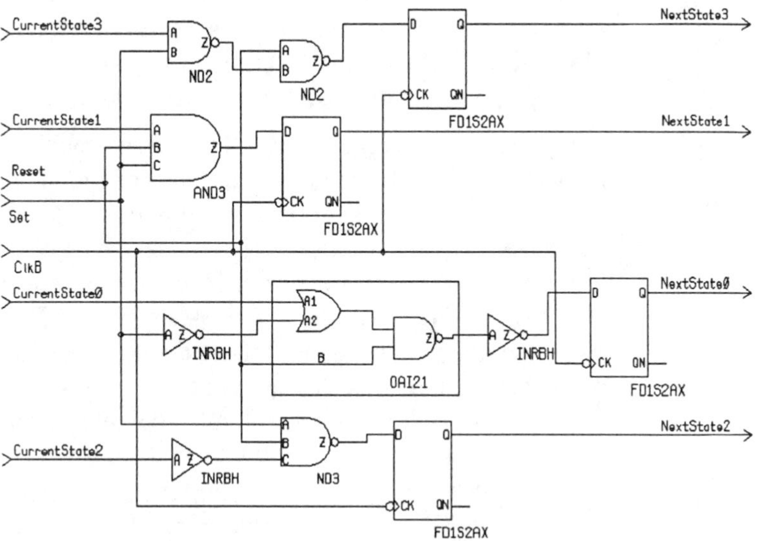

Figure 2-55 Not a synchronous preset and clear flip-flop.

From this example, it appears that all the inputs to *NextState*, the value 12, the value 5, and the variable *CurrentState*, should be multiplexed using appropriate select lines into the D-input of the inferred flip-flops for *NextState*. This is exactly what occurs as shown in the synthesized netlist in Figure 2-55. So then, how can we infer flip-flops with synchronous preset and clear? A synthesis system may provide a solution for this by providing a special option for directing the synthesis system to generate a synchronous preset clear flip-flop.

2.18 More on Blocking vs Non-blocking Assignments

In the previous sections, we have recommended that only non-blocking procedural assignments be used for modeling sequential logic (except for intermediate variables for which blocking assignments should be used) and that only blocking procedural assignments be used for modeling combinational logic. While these recommendations are followed in all examples in this text, in this section, we mix blocking and non-blocking assignments to illustrate the semantic differences, as it applies to synthesis, between the two kinds of procedural statements.

There is a difference between how non-blocking and blocking assignments are treated for synthesis because of the language semantic difference. In a blocking assignment, the assignment to the left-hand-side target completes before the next statement in the sequential block is executed (there is no difference between blocking and non-blocking if only one statement is present in the always statement). In a non-blocking assignment, the assignment to the left-hand-side target is scheduled for the end of the simulation cycle (assignment does not occur immediately) before the next statement is executed. Let us look at an example.

```
module FlagBits (ClockB, Strobe, Xflag, Mask,
                 RightShift, SelectFirst, CheckStop);
  input ClockB, Strobe, Xflag, Mask;
  output RightShift, SelectFirst, CheckStop;
  reg RightShift, SelectFirst, CheckStop;

  always @ (negedge ClockB)
  begin
    RightShift = RightShift & Strobe;   // Blocking
    SelectFirst <= RightShift | Xflag; // Non-blocking
    CheckStop <= SelectFirst ^ Mask;    // Non-blocking
  end
endmodule
// Synthesized netlist is shown in Figure 2-56.
```

The always statement has a sequential block with three assignment statements, the first one is a blocking procedural assignment and the next two are non-blocking assignments. Since all these assignments occur under the control of a clock edge, falling-edge-triggered flip-flops are synthe-

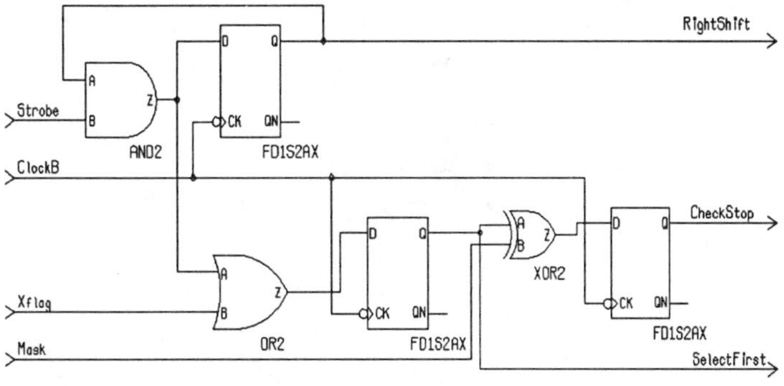

Figure 2-56 Non-blocking vs blocking procedural assignment.

sized for *RightShift*, *SelectFirst* and *CheckStop*. However, the difference is in the way the information is connected to the data input of these flip-flops. Because the assignment to *RightShift* is a blocking assignment, the new value of *RightShift* is available for use in the second assignment. This implies that the data input of the *RightShift* flip-flop should be used to gate into the data input of the *SelectFirst* flip-flop. Because *SelectFirst* is a non-blocking assignment, the use of *SelectFirst* in the third assignment refers to the old value of *SelectFirst*, not to the value being assigned in the second statement. Consequently, it is the flip-flop output of *SelectFirst* (old value) that feeds the data input of the *CheckStop* flip-flop. The difference explained can also be confirmed in the synthesized netlist shown in Figure 2-56.

Here is another example that highlights the difference between blocking and non-blocking assignments in synthesis.

```
module NonBlockingExample (ClockZ, Merge, ER, Xmit,
                           FDDI, Claim);
  input ClockZ, Merge, ER, Xmit, FDDI;
  output Claim;
  reg Claim;
  reg FCR;

  always @ (posedge ClockZ)
  begin
    FCR <= ER | Xmit;           // Assignment 1.
```

```
    if (Merge)
      Claim <= FCR & FDDI;       // Assignment 2.
    else
      Claim <= FDDI;
  end
endmodule
// Synthesized netlist is shown in Figure 2-57.
```

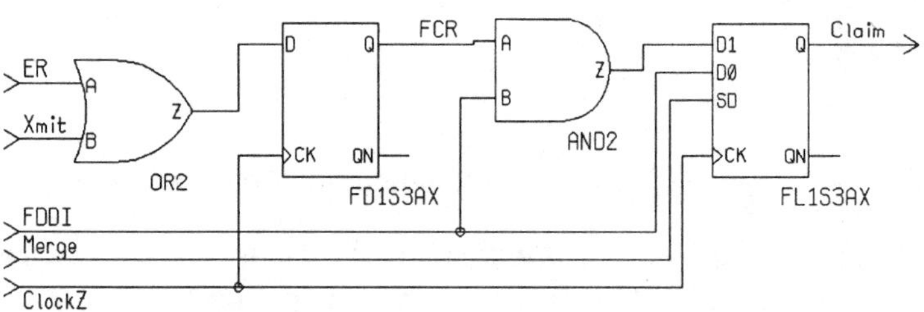

Figure 2-57 Non-blocking assignments.

There are three assignment statements in this example. Statements within the sequential block execute sequentially. However, the target of a non-blocking assignment is always assigned a value in the future (at the end of the current simulation time). Therefore in keeping with the language semantics of a non-blocking assignment, the use of *FCR* in assignment 2 is the old value of *FCR* and not the value assigned in assignment 1. Thus in the synthesized netlist, the output of the flip-flop for *FCR* is used to feed into the logic for *Claim*.

Let us now look at the same example when blocking procedural assignments are used.

```
module BlockingExample (ClockZ, Merge, ER, Xmit, FDDI,
                               Claim);
  input ClockZ, Merge, ER, Xmit, FDDI;
  output Claim;
  reg Claim;

  reg FCR;

  always @ (posedge ClockZ)
  begin
    FCR = ER | Xmit;             // Assignment 1.
```

```
      if (Merge)
        Claim = FCR & FDDI;          // Assignment 2.
      else
        Claim = FDDI;
    end
  endmodule
  // Synthesized netlist is shown in Figure 2-58.
```

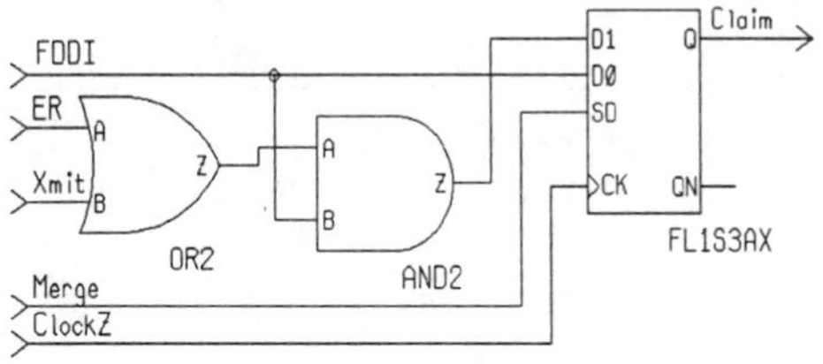

Figure 2-58 Blocking assignments.

In this case, the assignment to *FCR* must complete first before assignment 2 is done. Thus to mimic the language semantics, the right-hand-side expression of assignment 1 must be used to form the logic for the data for *Claim*. This is shown in the synthesized netlist. In addition, no flip-flop is inferred for *FCR* since its value is assigned and then used; the value of *FCR* does not have to be saved between different iterations of the always statement.

Chapter 5 explains the rationale behind the recommendation for using non-blocking assignments for sequential logic and for using blocking assignments for combinational logic; this is to prevent any possibility of a functional mismatch between the Verilog HDL model and its synthesized netlist. Note that this is only a recommendation; in many cases, it may be perfectly okay to use either of the two assignments, as long as the semantic differences are understood.

2.19 Functions

A function call represents combinational logic since a function call is part of an expression in Verilog HDL. A function call is synthesized by expanding the function call into in-line code. Any local variable declared within the function is treated as a pure temporary; such a variable gets synthesized as a wire.

Here is an example of a function call.

```
module FunctionCall (XBC, DataIn);
  output XBC;
  input [0:5] DataIn;

  function [0:2] CountOnes;
    input [0:5] A;
    integer K;
    begin
      CountOnes = 0;

      for (K = 0; K <= 5; K = K + 1)
        if (A[K])
          CountOnes = CountOnes + 1;
    end
  endfunction

  // If number of ones in DataIn is greater than 2,
  // return 1 in XBC.
  assign XBC = CountOnes (DataIn) > 2;
endmodule
// Synthesized netlist is shown in Figure 2-59.
```

After in-line expansion of the function call and further in-line expansion of the for-loop statement, the following code is obtained.

```
CountOnes = 0;
if (DataIn[0]) CountOnes = CountOnes + 1;
if (DataIn[1]) CountOnes = CountOnes + 1;
if (DataIn[2]) CountOnes = CountOnes + 1;
if (DataIn[3]) CountOnes = CountOnes + 1;
if (DataIn[4]) CountOnes = CountOnes + 1;
```

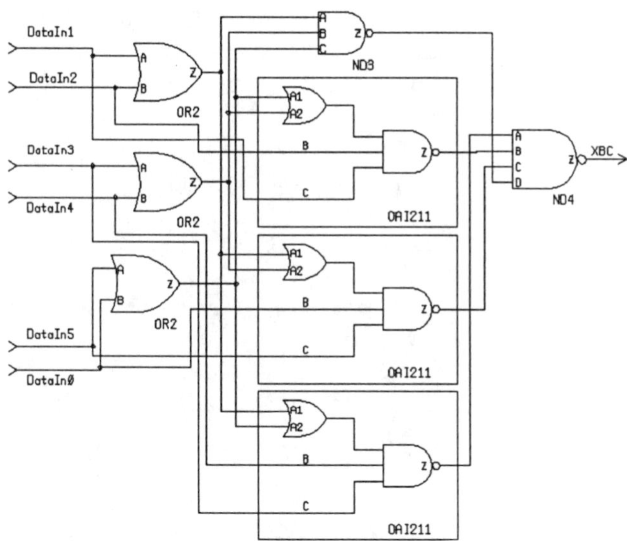

Figure 2-59 A function call example.

```
if (DataIn[5]) CountOnes = CountOnes + 1;
XBC = CountOnes > 2;
```

2.20 Tasks

A task call can represent either combinational logic or sequential logic depending on the context under which the task call occurs. By this, we mean that the output parameters of a task call may imply memory depending on the context in which they are assigned. For example, if a task call occurs in a clocked always statement (always statement with a clock event), then an output parameter in a task call may be synthesized as a flip-flop; this is determined by using the flip-flop inference rules. A synthesis system implements a task call by expanding the task call in-line with the rest of the code; in effect, no separate hierarchy for the task call is maintained.

Here is an example of a task call that represents pure combinational logic.

```
module CombTask (ShA, ShB, ShCarryIn, ShSum,
                 ShCarryOut);
  input [0:2] ShA, ShB;
  input ShCarryIn;
  output [0:2] ShSum;
  output ShCarryOut;
  reg [0:3] TempCarry;

  task AddOneBitWithCarry;
    input A, B, CarryIn;
    output Sum, CarryOut;
    begin
      Sum = A ^ B ^ CarryIn;
      CarryOut = A & B & CarryIn;
    end
  endtask

  always @ (ShA or ShB or ShCarryIn)
  begin: EXAMPLE
    integer J;

    TempCarry[0] = ShCarryIn;

    for (J = 0; J < 3; J = J + 1)
      AddOneBitWithCarry (ShA[J], ShB[J],
        TempCarry[J], ShSum[J], TempCarry[J+1]);
  end

  assign ShCarryOut = TempCarry[3];
endmodule
// Synthesized netlist is shown in Figure 2-60.
```

After in-line expansion of the task call and the for-loop statement by the synthesis tool, the following code is obtained.

```
TempCarry[0] = ShCarryIn;
ShSum[0] = ShA[0] ^ ShB[0] ^ TempCarry[0];
TempCarry[1] = ShA [0] & ShB[0] & TempCarry[0];
ShSum[1] = ShA[1] ^ ShB[1] ^ TempCarry[1];
TempCarry[2] = ShA[1] & ShB[1] & TempCarry[1];
ShSum[2] = ShA[2] ^ ShB[2] ^ TempCarry[2];
```

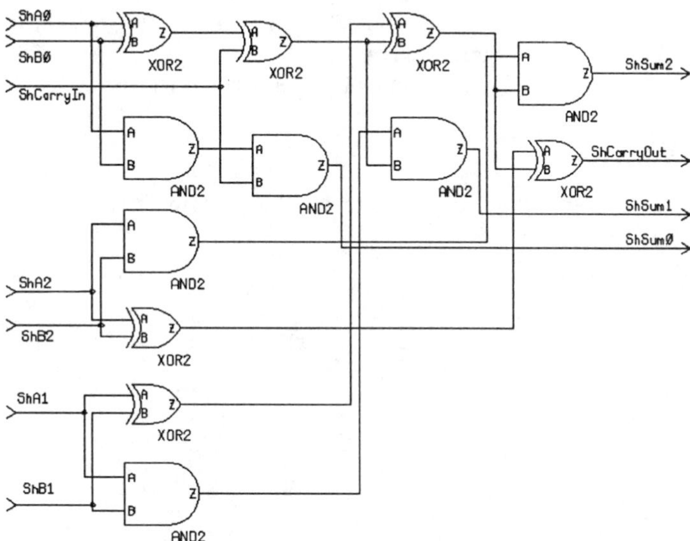

Figure 2-60 A task call example: combinational logic.

```
TempCarry[3] = ShA[2] & ShB[2] & TempCarry[2];
ShCarryOut = TempCarry[3];
```

Next is an example of a task call that occurs under the control of a clock edge.

```
module SynTask (ByteIn, ClockFa, ByteOut);
  input [3:0] ByteIn;
  input ClockFa;
  output [3:0] ByteOut;

  task ReverseByte;
    input [3:0] A;
    output [3:0] Z;
    integer J;
    begin
      for (J = 3; J >= 0; J = J - 1)
        Z[J] = A[3-J];
    end
  endtask
```

```
  always @ (negedge ClockFa)
    ReverseByte (ByteIn, ByteOut);
endmodule
// Synthesized netlist is shown in Figure 2-61.
```

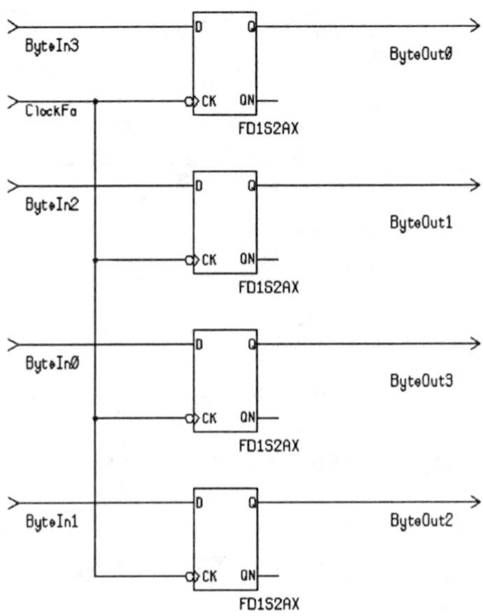

Figure 2-61 A task call example: synchronous logic.

In this example, variable *ByteOut* is assigned a value under the control of clock *ClockFa*; thus, *ByteOut* gets synthesized as a flip-flop. The code after in-line expansion of the task call looks like this.

```
ByteOut[3] = ByteIn[0];
ByteOut[2] = ByteIn[1];
ByteOut[1] = ByteIn[2];
ByteOut[0] = ByteIn[3];
```

2.21 Using Values x and z

Verilog HDL has two non-logical values: x (unknown) and z (high-impedance). In this section, we specify the domain under which these values can be used for synthesis. Use caution when using these values in a synthesis model as they can potentially cause a functional mismatch between the design model and the synthesized netlist.

2.21.1 The Value x

The value x can be assigned to any variable in an assignment statement. In such a case, x is treated as a don't-care for synthesis purposes. A synthesis system may intelligently select either a logic-0 or a logic-1 for the value x that leads to optimal logic.

```
Reset = 'bx;   // Assign a don't-care value to Reset.
  // Synthesis system will automatically select
  // logic-0 or logic-1.
```

When value x is used in a case item of a case statement (not casex, casez), the branch corresponding to that case item is considered never to execute for synthesis purposes.

```
case (In)
  2'bx : Out = In;      // This branch will never occur for
                        // synthesis.
  default : Out = ~ In;
endcase
```

Thus a functional mismatch may occur; a synthesis tool may report a warning in such a case. Avoid using x in a case item of a case statement (not casex, casez).

2.21.2 The Value z

The value z is used to generate a three-state gate. The value z can be assigned to a variable in an assignment statement; however for synthesis, such an assignment must occur under the control of a condition, either in an `if` statement, or in a case statement. Here is an example.

```
module ThreeState (Ready, DataInA, DataInB, Select1);
  input Ready, DataInA, DataInB;
  output Select1;
  reg Select1;

  always @ (Ready or DataInA or DataInB)
    if (Ready)
      Select1 = 1'bz;
    else
      Select1 = DataInA & DataInB;
endmodule
// Synthesized netlist is shown in Figure 2-62.
```

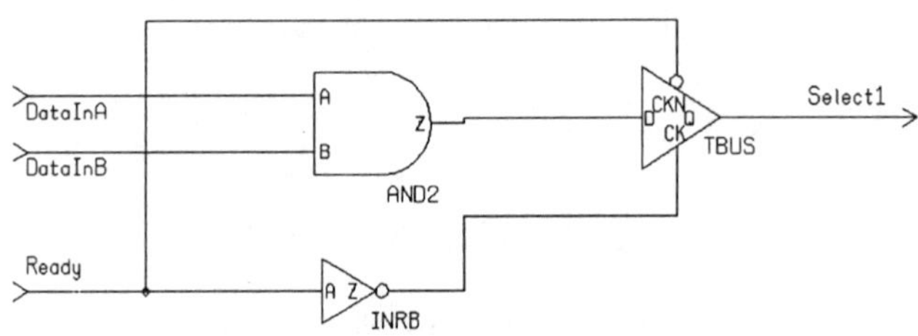

Figure 2-62 A conditional z value assignment produces a three-state gate.

A three-state gate can also be obtained by assigning the value z in a conditional expression, as shown in the next example.

```
module CondExprThreeState (Dnt, GateCtrl, Vcs);
  input Dnt, GateCtrl;
  output Vcs;

  assign Vcs = GateCtrl ? Dnt : 1'bz;
endmodule
// Synthesized netlist is shown in Figure 2-63.
```

Furthermore, when the value z is used in a case item of a case statement (not casez, casex), the branch corresponding to the case item is considered as never to execute for synthesis purposes.

```
case (Select)
  2'b1z : DBus = | AFlow;     // This branch will never
```

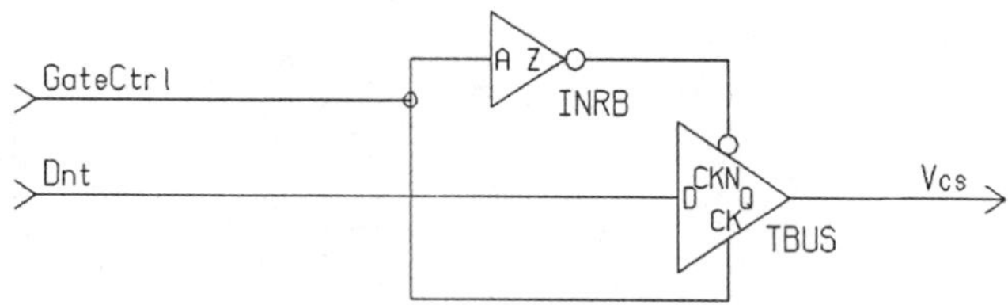

Figure 2-63 Three-state gate using a conditional expression.

```
                                    // execute for synthesis.
  2'b11 : DBus = ^ AFlow;
  default : DBus = & AFlow;
endcase
```

Thus a functional mismatch may occur in such a case; a good synthesis tool will report a warning. A good rule to follow is to simply avoid using the value z in a case item of a case statement (not casex, casez).

If a variable is assigned a value z in an always statement in which the variable is also inferred as a flip-flop, then it becomes necessary to save the enabling logic of the three-state also in a flip-flop. Here is the same example as above except that the always statement is controlled by a clock event.

```
module ThreeStateExtraFF (Clock, Ready, DataInA,
                          DataInB, Select1);
  input Clock, Ready, DataInA, DataInB;
  output Select1;
  reg Select1;

  always @ (posedge Clock)
    if (Ready)
      Select1 <= 'bz;
    else
      Select1 <= DataInA & DataInB;
endmodule
// Synthesized netlist is shown in Figure 2-64.
```

Notice that two flip-flops are synthesized, one for *Select1* and one for the condition *Ready*. If the extra flip-flop for *Ready* is not desired, the model should be rewritten by separating the three-state logic and the flip-flop in-

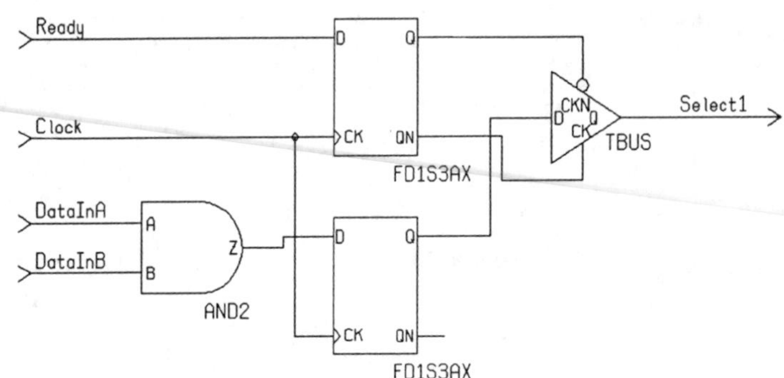

Figure 2-64 Extra flip-flop holding the three-state enable value.

ferencing logic into two separate always statement as shown next in module *ThreeStateNoExtraFF*. The behavior of the two modules, *ThreeStateExtraFF* and *ThreeStateNoExtraFF* is different; in the former case, the output is directly dependent on *Clock*, in the latter case, output is not directly dependent on the *Clock*, but is directly dependent on *Ready*.

```
module ThreeStateNoExtraFF (Clock, Ready, DataInA,
                                DataInB, Select1);
  input Clock, Ready, DataInA, DataInB;
  output Select1;
  reg Select1, TempSelect1;

  // Sequential logic:
  always @ (posedge Clock)
    TempSelect1 = DataInA & DataInB;

  // Combinational logic:
  always @ (TempSelect1 or Ready)
    if (Ready)
      Select1 = 'bz;
    else
      Select1 = TempSelect1;
endmodule
// Synthesized netlist is shown in Figure 2-65.
```

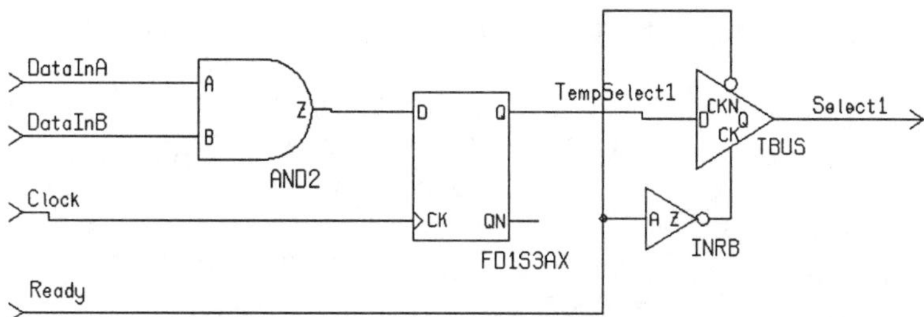

Figure 2-65 No extra flip-flop.

Notice that in this case a temporary variable *TempSelect1* is introduced that is used to communicate between the first always statement (sequential part) with the second always statement (combinational part). Only one flip-flop is synthesized for *TempSelect1*.

2.22 Gate Level Modeling

Gate level primitives can be instantiated in a model using gate instantiation. The following gate level primitives are supported for synthesis.

```
and, nand, or, nor, not, xor, xnor, buf,
bufif0, bufif1, notif0, notif1
```

Synthesizing a gate primitive simply generates logic based on the gate behavior, which eventually gets mapped to the target technology. Synthesizing any of the last four listed primitives (three-state gate primitives), synthesizes a three-state gate in the appropriate target technology with additional combinational logic to support the behavior of the three-state gate. Here is an example that drives the `and` of two inputs onto a bus if control is 1, else it drives the `or` of the two inputs.

```
module GateLevel (A, B, Ctrl, Zbus);
  input A, B, Ctrl;
  output Zbus;
  // Not necessary to declare nets AndOut and OrOut.
  // The instance names, A1, O1, etc. are also optional
  // but are recommended for simulation debugging.
```

```
    and A1 (AndOut, A, B); // First terminal is output,
                           // other two are inputs.
    or O1 (OrOut, A, B);
    bufif0 B1 (Zbus, AndOut, Ctrl);   // First terminal is
        // output, second terminal is input, and third
        // terminal is control.
    bufif0 B2 (Zbus, OrOut, ! Ctrl);
endmodule
// Synthesized netlist is shown in Figure 2-66.
```

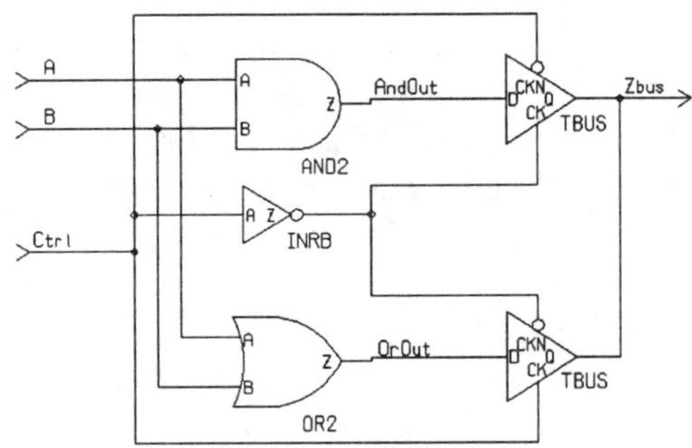

Figure 2-66 Gate instantiations.

Delays, if any, in gate instantiations are ignored by a synthesis system. This can potentially lead to functional mismatches between the Verilog HDL model and the synthesized netlist.

2.23 Module Instantiation Statement

A module instantiation statement can be written within a module declaration. A synthesis system treats such a module instance as a black box and does not take further action, that is, the module instance appears in the synthesized netlist as if it were a primitive component. Here is an example of a full-adder module that contains one module instantiation statement. Notice that in the synthesized netlist, shown in Figure 2-67, the module *MyXor* appears just as it is described in the top level module *FullAdderMix*.

```
module FullAdderMix (A, B, CarryIn, Sum, CarryOut);
  input A, B, CarryIn;
  output Sum, CarryOut;
  wire Sft;                   // Sft need not be declared.

  MyXor X1 (.In0(A), .In1(B), .Out(Sft));

  assign CarryOut = A & B & CarryIn;
  assign Sum = Sft ^ CarryIn;
endmodule
// Synthesized netlist is shown in Figure 2-67.
```

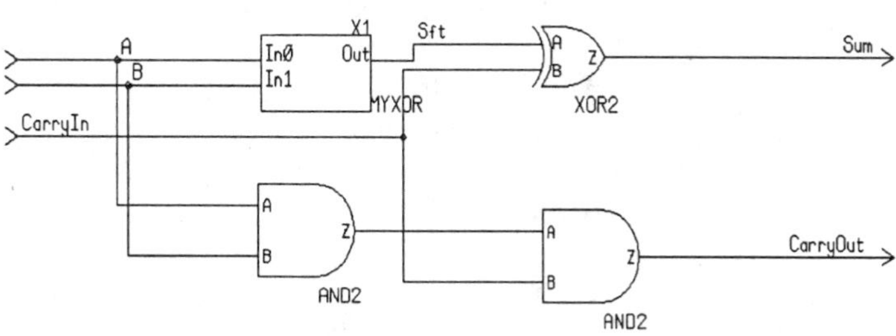

Figure 2-67 A module instance mixed with behavior.

2.23.1 Using Predefined Blocks

Module instantiation statements are often used to instantiate predefined blocks when a designer is not satisfied with the quality of circuits produced by a synthesis tool. A designer may also have a library of predefined blocks such as memories. In such a case, the designer may prefer to instantiate a predefined block using a module instantiation statement instead of writing a behavioral description for the block. Thus a module instantiation statement provides flexibility in controlling the logic that is synthesized, and allows mixing of one or more predefined blocks as well.

Instantiating User-built Multipliers

As a first example, consider the case where a designer is not happy with the multiplication logic generated by a synthesis tool. This logic might have been generated from the following code.

```
module MultiplyAndReduce (OpdA, OpdB, ReducedResult);
  input [1:0] OpdA, OpdB;
  output ReducedResult;
  wire [3:0] Test;

  assign Test = OpdA * OpdB;       // Multiply operator.
  assign ReducedResult = & Test;
endmodule
```

In this example, the designer may instantiate a predefined multiplier as follows.

```
module PreDefMultiplyAndReduce (OpdA, OpdB,
                                       ReducedResult);
  input [1:0] OpdA, OpdB;
  output ReducedResult;

  wire [3:0] Test;

  MyMult M1 (.Input1 (OpdA), .Input2 (OpdB),
            .Result (Test));

  assign ReducedResult = & Test;
endmodule
// Synthesized netlist is shown in Figure 2-68.
```

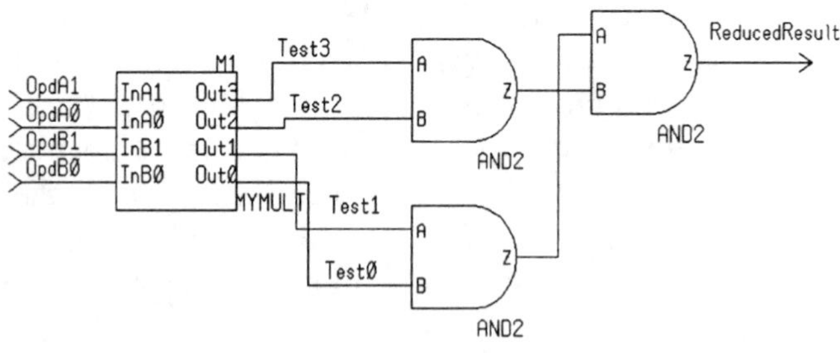

Figure 2-68 Instantiating a predefined multiplier.

Instantiating User-specific Flip-flops

A flip-flop is yet another case where a designer may want to control the type of flip-flop being generated. Normally a flip-flop is inferred for a variable that is assigned a value within a clocked always statement. However, such a synthesized flip-flop may not be optimal for the design. A designer may want to use a custom-made flip-flop instead of the flip-flop generated by the synthesis tool. This can be modeled again by instantiating the predefined flip-flop as a module instance. Here is an example.

```
module PreDefFlipFlop (Dclock, Request, DayP,
                       DelS, Fop);
  input Dclock, Request, DayP, DelS;
  output Fop;
  reg Fop;
  wire NewRequest;                        // Optional.

  MyFlipFlop LabelF1 (.Data (Request), .Clock (Dclock),
                      .Q (NewRequest));
// The above module instantiation statement replaces the
// following always statement:
  // always @ (posedge Dclock)
  //   NewRequest = Request;

  always @ (NewRequest or DayP or DelS)
    if (NewRequest)
      Fop = DayP;
    else
      Fop = DelS;
endmodule
// Synthesized netlist is shown in Figure 2-69.
```

Here is another example. This is a 3-bit up-down counter that shows how a pre-built D-type flip-flop is used along with its remaining behavior. The key statements that are necessary to be added are the module instantiation statements. With such a model, a synthesis system retains the pre-built component in the synthesized design to achieve the desired result; this is shown in the synthesized netlist.

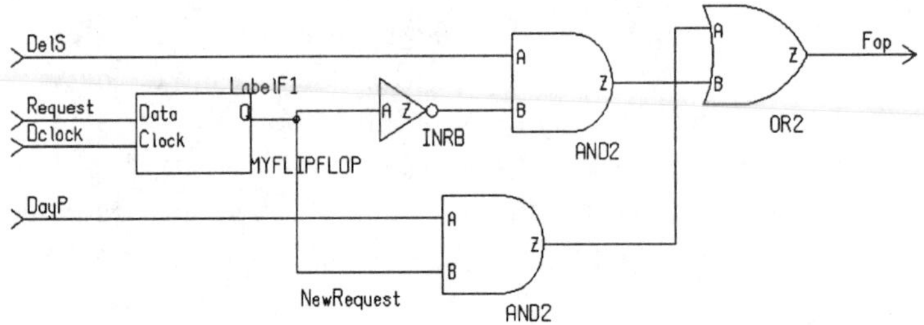

Figure 2-69 Instantiating a predefined flip-flop.

```
module UpDownCntr (ClkA, UpDown, PresetClear, Q0, Q1,
                    Q2);
  input ClkA, UpDown, PresetClear;
  output Q0, Q1, Q2;
  wire Bit01, Bit11, Bit12, Bit13, Qn0, Qn1, Qn2;

  assign Bit01 = UpDown ^ Q0;
  assign Bit11 = Bit01 ^ Qn1;
  assign Bit12 = UpDown ^ Q1;
  assign Bit13 = Bit01 | Bit12;
  assign Bit21 = Bit13 ^ Qn2;

  SpecialFF
    Lq0 (.D(Qn0), .Clk(ClkA), .PreClr(PresetClear),
          .Q(Q0), .Qbar(Qn0)),
    Lq1 (.D(Bit11), .Clk(ClkA), .PreClr(PresetClear),
          .Q(Q1), .Qbar(Qn1)),
    Lq2 (.D(Bit21), .Clk(ClkA), .PreClr(PresetClear),
          .Q(Q2), .Qbar(Qn2));
endmodule
// Synthesized netlist is shown in Figure 2-70.
```

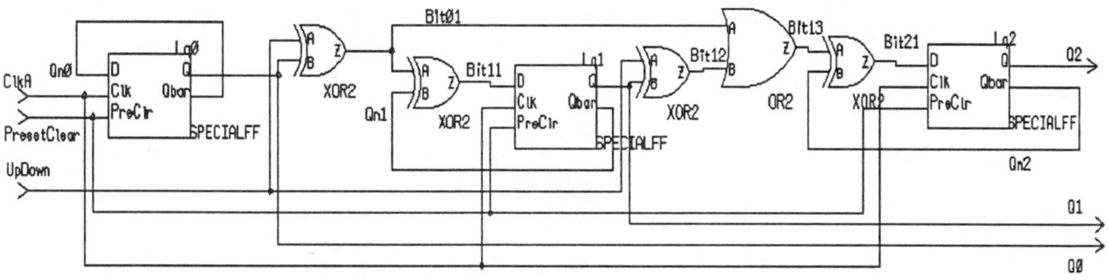

Figure 2-70 Using a special flip-flop.

2.24 Parameterized Designs

Parameters in Verilog HDL provide a powerful mechanism to model parameterized designs. Here is a simple example of an *N*-bit register.

```
module NbitRegister (Data, Clock, Q);
  parameter N = 3;
  input [N-1:0] Data;
  input Clock;
  output [N-1:0] Q;
  reg [N-1:0] Q;

  always @ (negedge Clock)
    Q <= Data;
endmodule
// Synthesized netlist is shown in Figure 2-71.
```

The module *NbitRegister* when synthesized produces a 3-bit register. The module is a parameterized module since the size of the register has been specified using a parameter which can be modified easily or overwritten by instantiating it from another module. For example, if a 4-bit register is required, one way is to just change *N* in the module *NbitRegister* to 4 and resynthesize. The other alternative is to instantiate *NbitRegister* in a different module and specify a new value for *N*; this approach has the advantage that the parameterized module *NbitRegister* does not have to be modified. Here is a module that instantiates two 2-bit registers. The new parameter values, that is, the new values for *N*, are specified using the # symbol.

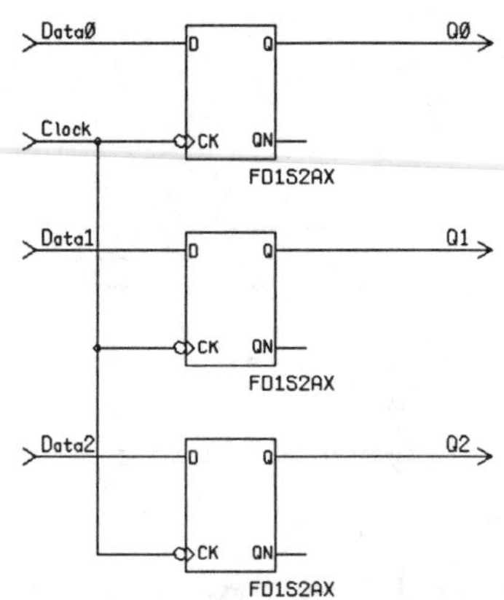

Figure 2-71 A parameterized register.

```
module ResolveBuses (BusA, BusB, BusControl, Clock,
                     FinalBus);
  parameter NBITS = 2;
  input [NBITS:1] BusA, BusB;
  input BusControl, Clock;
  output [NBITS:1] FinalBus;

  wire [NBITS:1] SavedA, SavedB;

  RegisterFile # (NBITS) RfOne (.Data(BusA),
        .Clock(Clock), .Q(SavedA));
  RegisterFile # (NBITS) RfTwo (.Data(BusB),
        .Clock(Clock), .Q(SavedB));

  assign FinalBus = BusControl ? SavedA : SavedB;
endmodule
// Synthesized netlist is shown in Figure 2-72.
```

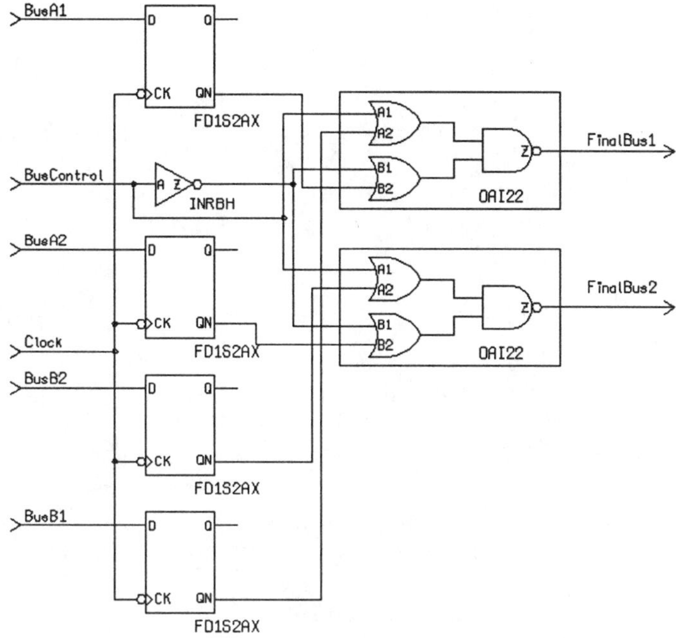

Figure 2-72 Instantiating a parameterized register.

Chapter 3 shows many more modeling examples that show the collective usage of many Verilog HDL constructs.

❑

CHAPTER

3

MODELING EXAMPLES

In Chapter 2, we looked at the synthesis of Verilog HDL statements into gates. In this chapter we look at an orthogonal view, that is the task of modeling hardware elements for synthesis and how Verilog HDL can be used to achieve this. As before, we show both the Verilog HDL model and the schematic for the synthesized output.

This chapter also provides a number of more complicated Verilog HDL synthesis examples. These models illustrate the usage of Verilog HDL constructs collectively to model a design that can be synthesized.

Sequential logic and combinational logic can be synthesized from a Verilog HDL description. There are two main styles for describing combinational logic:

i. Using continuous assignment statements: This is the most natural style, since it explicitly shows the parallelism in the hardware. It also implicitly shows the structure.

ii. Using procedural assignment statements in a sequential block of an always statement: The statements describe the composition of intermediate values within a combinational logic block; this is because the language semantics specify that all statements in a sequential block execute sequentially.

Sequential logic elements, that is, flip-flops and latches, can be inferred by writing statements within an always statement using styles described in Chapter 2. It is best not to synthesize a memory as a two-dimensional array of flip-flops because this is an inefficient way to implement a memory. The best way to create a memory is to instantiate a predefined memory block using a module instantiation statement.

3.1 Modeling Combinational Logic

One good approach for describing combinational logic is to use continuous assignment statements. An always statement can also be used to describe combinational logic; however, the synthesized logic may not be apparent from the description. If combinational logic is described using continuous assignment statements, then the synthesized logic is implicit in the description. Consider the following model of a built-in self-test cell.

```
module BistCell (B0, B1, D0, D1, Z);
  input B0, B1, D0, D1;
  output Z;
  wire S1, S2, S3, S4;

  assign S1 = ~ (B0 & D1);
  assign S2 = ~ (D0 & B1);
  assign S3 = ~ (S2 | S1);
  assign S4 = S2 & S1;
  assign Z = ~ (S4 | S3);
endmodule
// Synthesized netlist is shown in Figure 3-1.
```

Notice the structure of the synthesized circuit is very similar to that of the continuous assignment statements.

Here is the same model, but this time the cell is described using an always statement.

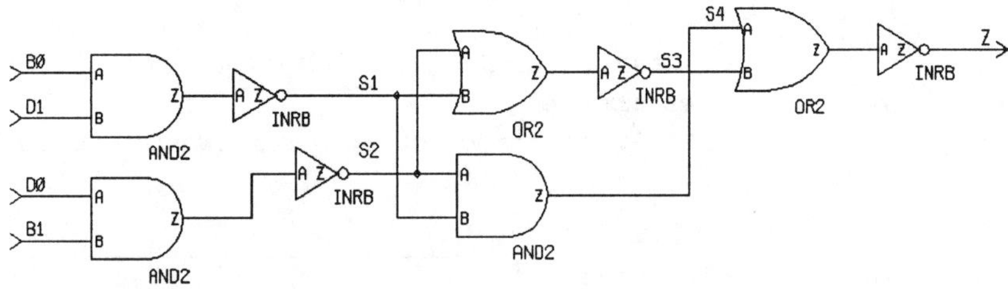

Figure 3-1 Combinational logic from continuous assignments.

```
module BistCellReg (B0, B1, D0, D1, Z);
  input B0, B1, D0, D1;
  output Z;
  reg Z;

  reg S1, S2, S3;

  always @(B0 or D0 or B1 or D1)
  begin
    S1 = ~ (B0 & D1);
    S2 = ~ (D0 & B1);
    S3 = ~ (S2 | S1);
    S1 = S2 & S1;
     Z = ~ (S1 | S3);
  end
endmodule
```

In module *BistCell*, each wire declared corresponded to a unique wire in the synthesized netlist. Not so with reg variable *S1* in module *BistCellReg*. Notice that the variable *S1* is used as a temporary in more than one place and does not represent one wire. The synthesized circuit still remains the same as that shown in Figure 3-1; however, the one-to-one mapping between the variables in the always statement and the nets in the synthesized netlist is not present.

Here is an example of a combinational logic model of a 2-to-1 multiplexer with an enable.

```
module Mux2To1 (A, B, Select, Enable, ZeeQ);
  input [1:0] A, B;
  input Select, Enable;
```

```
  output [1:0] ZeeQ;

  assign ZeeQ = (Enable) ? (Select ? A : B) : 'bz;
endmodule
// Synthesized netlist is shown in Figure 3-2.
```

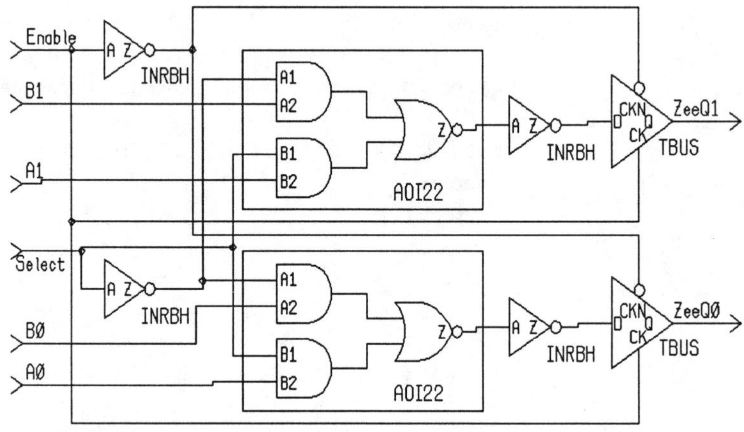

Figure 3-2 A 2-to-1 multiplexer.

3.2 Modeling Sequential Logic

The following sequential logic elements can be modeled.

i. flip-flop: see section 2.17.

ii. flip-flop with asynchronous preset and or clear: see section 2.17.

iii. flip-flop with synchronous preset and or clear: see section 2.17.

iv. latch: see section 2.15.

v. latch with asynchronous preset and or clear: see section 2.15.

3.3 Modeling a Memory

A memory is best modeled as a component. Typically, synthesis tools are not efficient at designing a memory. More traditional techniques are generally used to build a memory. Once having built this module, it can then be instantiated in a synthesis model as a component using the module instantiation statement.

```
module ROM (Clock, OutEnable, Address, Q, Qbar);
  input Clock, OutEnable;
  input [M-1:0] Address;
  output [N-1:0] Q, Qbar;

  // Memory description here (might not be
  // synthesizable).
  . . .
endmodule

module MyModule ( . . . );
  wire Clk, Enable;
  wire [M-1:0] Abus;
  wire [N-1:0] Dbus;

  ROM R1 (.Clock(Clk), .OutEnable(Enable),
          .Address(Abus), .Q(Dbus), .Qbar());
  . . .
endmodule
```

A register file can be modeled as a two-dimensional reg variable (a two-dimensional reg variable is referred to as memory in Verilog HDL), which can then be synthesized. Here is an example of a register file.

```
module RegFileWithMemory (Clk, ReadWrite, Index,
                          DataIn, DataOut);
  parameter N = 2, M = 2;
  input Clk, ReadWrite;
  input [1:N] Index;      // Range need not be that large.
  input [0:M-1] DataIn;
  output [0:M-1] DataOut;
  reg [0:M-1] DataOut;
```

```
      reg [0:M-1] RegFile [0:N-1];

      always @ (negedge Clk)
        if (ReadWrite)
          DataOut <= RegFile[Index];
        else
          RegFile[Index] <= DataIn;
    endmodule
    // Synthesized netlist of a 2-by-2 register file is
    // shown in Figure 3-3.
```

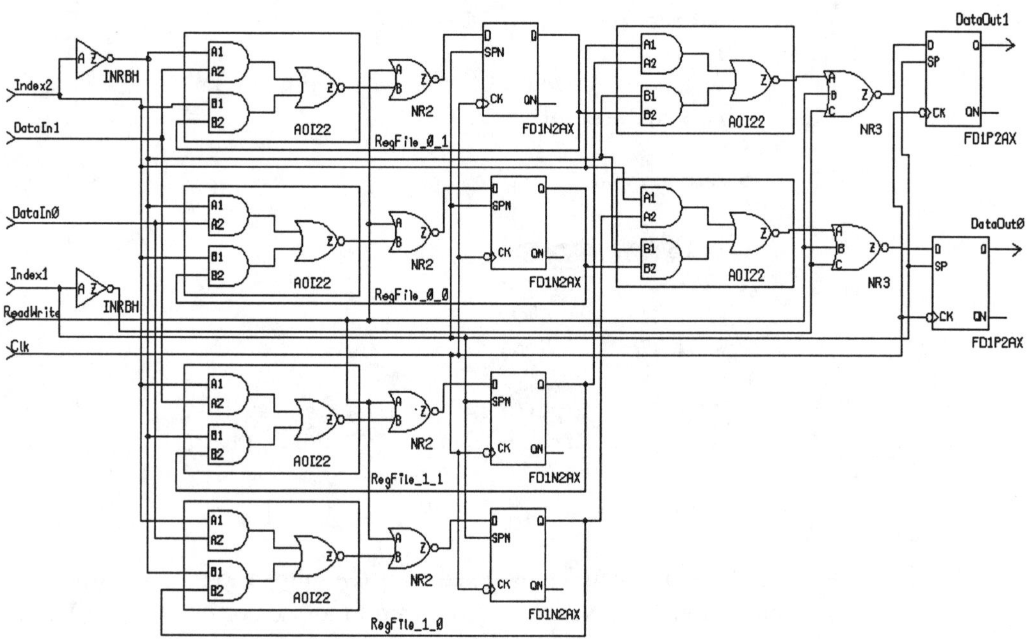

Figure 3-3 A 2-by-2 register file.

Note that there are a total of six flip-flops synthesized, four for the register file *RegFile* and two for *DataOut*.

3.4 Writing Boolean Equations

Boolean equations represent combinational logic. Boolean equations are best represented using continuous assignment statements. Here is an example of a Gray code to binary code convertor using boolean equations.

```
A B C  Binary Code
0 0 0  0 0 0
0 0 1  0 0 1
0 1 1  0 1 0
0 1 0  0 1 1
1 1 0  1 0 0
1 1 1  1 0 1
1 0 1  1 1 0
1 0 0  1 1 1
```

```
module GrayToBinary (A, B, C, Bc0, Bc1, Bc2);
  input A, B, C;
  output Bc0, Bc1, Bc2;
  wire NotA, NotB, NotC;

  assign NotC = ~ C;
  assign NotB = ~ B;
  assign NotA = ~ A;

  assign Bc0 = (A & B & NotC) | (A & B & C) |
               (A & NotB & C) | (A & NotB & NotC);
  assign Bc1 = (NotA & B & C) | (NotA & B & NotC) |
               (A & NotB & C) | (A & NotB & NotC);
  assign Bc2 = (NotA & NotB & C) | (NotA & B & NotC) |
               (A & B & C) | (A & NotB & NotC);
endmodule
// Synthesized netlist is shown in Figure 3-4.
```

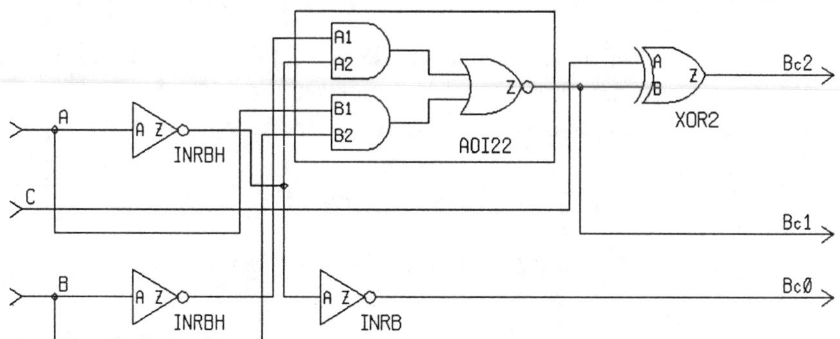

Figure 3-4 Gray to binary logic.

3.5 Modeling a Finite State Machine

3.5.1 Moore FSM

In a Moore finite state machine, the output of the circuit is dependent only on the state of the machine and not on its inputs. This is described pictorially in Figure 3-5. Since the outputs are dependent only on the state, a good way to describe a Moore machine is to use an always statement with a case statement. The case statement is used to switch between the various states and the output logic for each state is described in the appropriate branch. The always statement can have the clock event in its event list to indicate that it is a clocked always statement. This models the condition of a finite state machine going from state to state synchronously on every clock edge. The machine state itself is modeled using a reg variable (a variable of reg data type).

Here is an example of a Moore finite state machine. A reg variable *MooreState* is used to model the machine state which can have either of the four states. The event list indicates that the state transitions occur synchronously on every rising clock edge.

```
module MooreFSM (A, ClkM, Z);
  input A, ClkM;
  output Z;
```

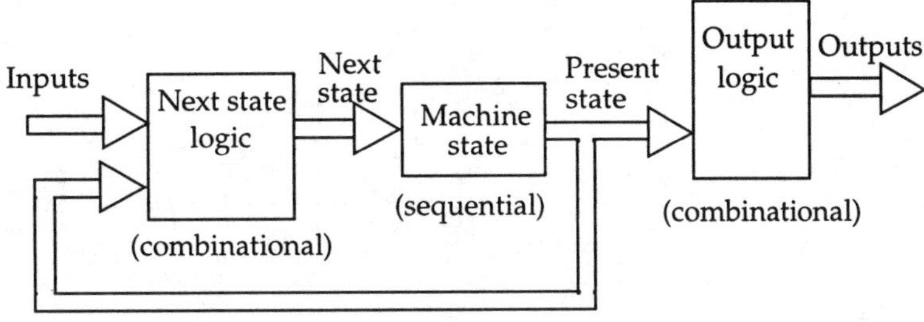

Figure 3-5 A Moore finite state machine.

```
  reg Z;

  parameter S0 = 0, S1 = 1, S2 = 2, S3 = 3;
  reg [0:1] MooreState;

  always @ (posedge ClkM)
    case (MooreState)
      S0 :
        begin
          Z <= 1;
          MooreState <= (! A) ? S0 : S2;
        end
      S1 :
        begin
          Z <= 0;
          MooreState <= (! A) ? S0 : S2;
        end
      S2 :
        begin
          Z <= 0;
          MooreState <= (! A) ? S2 : S3;
        end
      S3:
        begin
          Z <= 1;
          MooreState <= (! A) ? S1 : S3;
        end
    endcase
endmodule
// Synthesized netlist is shown in Figure 3-6.
```

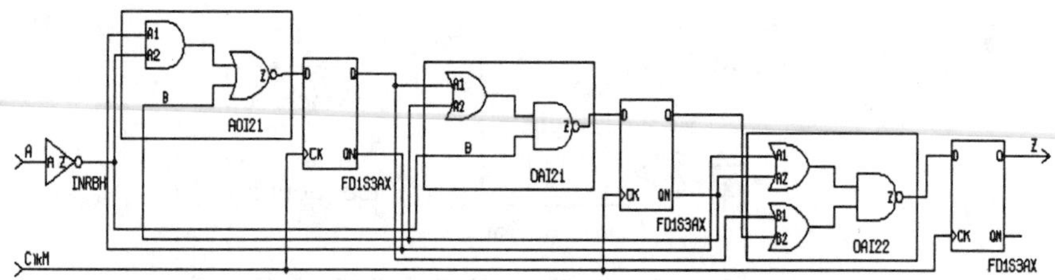

Figure 3-6 The synthesized netlist for the Moore FSM model.

When this model is synthesized, three flip-flops are inferred; two to hold the value of the machine state (*MooreState*) and one for the output *Z*. States are encoded using sequential state assignment.

In the previous example, the output is also saved in a flip-flop. What if a non-latched output is required? In this case, the assignments to *Z* can be separated out into a second always statement, as shown in the model next.

```
module MooreFSM2 (A, ClkM, Z);
  input A, ClkM;
  output Z;
  reg Z;

  parameter S0 = 0, S1 = 1, S2 = 2, S3 = 3;
  reg [0:1] MooreState;

  always @ (posedge ClkM)
    case (MooreState)
      S0 : MooreState <= (! A) ? S0 : S2;
      S1 : MooreState <= (! A) ? S0 : S2;
      S2 : MooreState <= (! A) ? S2 : S3;
      S3 : MooreState <= (! A) ? S1 : S3;
    endcase

  // Shows clearly that output is dependent on
  // only state.
  always @ (MooreState)
    case (MooreState)
      S0 : Z = 1;
      S1 : Z = 0;
      S2 : Z = 0;
```

```
        S3 : Z = 1;
      endcase
    endmodule
    // Synthesized netlist is shown in Figure 3-7.
```

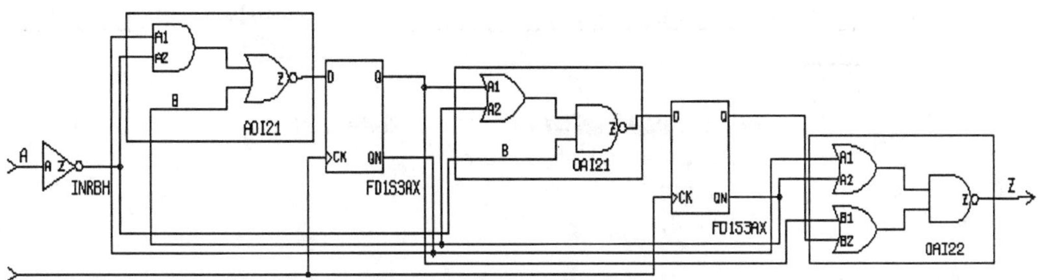

Figure 3-7 No latched output.

3.5.2 Mealy FSM

In a Mealy finite state machine, the output is dependent both on the machine state as well as on the inputs to the finite state machine. This is shown pictorially in Figure 3-8. Notice that in this case, outputs can change asynchronously with respect to clock.

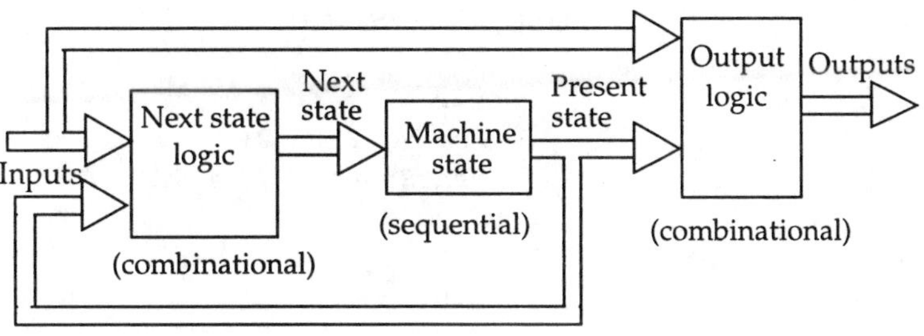

Figure 3-8 A Mealy finite state machine.

One of the best ways of describing a Mealy finite state machine is by using two always statements, one for describing the sequential logic, and one for describing the combinational logic (this includes both next state logic and output logic). It is necessary to do this since any changes on inputs directly affect the outputs used to describe the combinational logic. The state of the machine is modeled using a reg variable.

Here is an example of a Mealy finite state machine. Variable *MealyState* holds the machine state, while *NextState* is used to pass information from the combinational logic always statement to the sequential logic always statement. Input *Reset* asynchronously resets the state to *ST0*.

```
module MealyFSM (A, ClkB, Reset, Z);
  input A, ClkB, Reset;
  output Z;
  reg Z;

  parameter ST0 = 4'b00, ST1 = 4'b01, ST2 = 4'b10;
  reg [0:1] MealyState, NextState;

  // Sequential logic:
  always @ (posedge Reset or posedge ClkB)
    if (Reset)
      MealyState <= ST0;
    else
      MealyState <= NextState;

  // Combinational logic:
  always @ (MealyState or A)
    case (MealyState)
      ST0 :
        begin
          Z = (A) ? 1 : 0;
          NextState = (A) ? ST2 : ST0;
        end
      ST1 :
        begin
          Z = (A) ? 1 : 0;
          NextState = (A) ? ST0 : ST1;
        end
      ST2 :
        begin
          Z = 0;
          NextState = (A) ? ST1 : ST2;
        end
      default : // default behavior; required, else
```

```
            // latches are inferred for Z and NextState.
      begin
        Z = 0; NextState = ST0;
      end
    endcase
endmodule
// Synthesized netlist is shown in Figure 3-9.
```

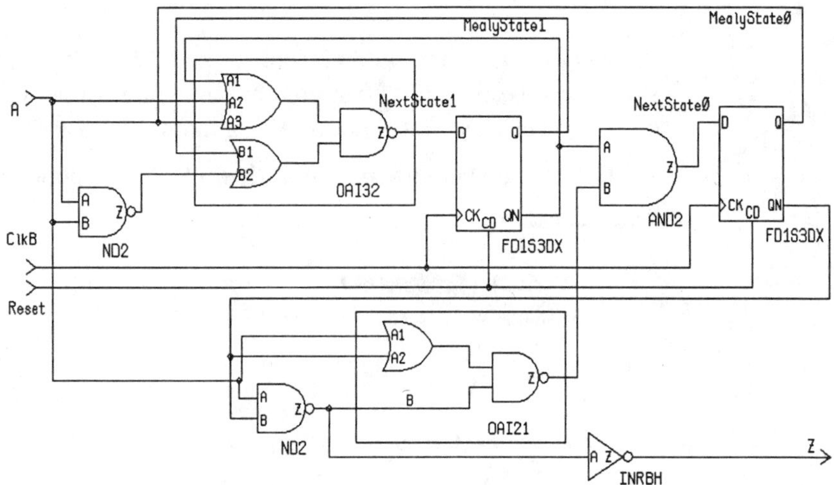

Figure 3-9 The synthesized netlist for the Mealy FSM example.

Two flip-flops are inferred to hold the value of the variable *MealyState* with the specified state assignment. The default branch in the case statement can be avoided by specifying the case statement as "full case", as shown next.

```
always @ (MealyState or A)
  case (MealyState)     // synthesis full_case
    ST0 :
      begin
        Z = (A) ? 1 : 0;
        NextState = (A) ? ST2 : ST0;
      end
    ST1 :
      begin
```

```
        Z = (A) ? 1 : 0;
        NextState = (A) ? ST0 : ST1;
      end
    ST2 :
      begin
        Z = 0;
        NextState = (A) ? ST1 : ST2;
      end
  endcase
```

In this case, no latches are inferred for *Z* and *NextState* since the full_case synthesis directive states that no other case item values can occur. However, the preferred style for not inferring latches is to use the default branch.

Here is another example of a Mealy FSM, this one uses one-hot state encoding.

```
module MealyFSM2 (A, ClkC, Reset, Z);
  input A, ClkC, Reset;
  output Z;
  reg Z;

  parameter ST0 = 2'd0, ST1 = 2'd1, ST2 = 2'd2;
  reg [0:2] NextState, MealyState;

  // Sequential logic:
  always @ (posedge Reset or posedge ClkC)
    if (Reset)
    begin
      MealyState <= 0;
      MealyState[ST0] <= 1'b1;
    end
    else
      MealyState <= NextState;

  // Combinational logic:
  always @ (MealyState or A)
  begin
    NextState = 3'b0;          // Default assignment.
    Z = 1'b0;

    case (1'b1)
      MealyState[ST0]:
```

```
        if (A)
        begin
          Z = 1'b1;
          NextState[ST2] = 1'b1;
        end
        else
          NextState[ST0] = 1'b1;
      MealyState[ST1]:
        if (A)
        begin
          Z = 1'b1;
          NextState[ST0] = 1'b1;
        end
        else
          NextState[ST1] = 1'b1;
      MealyState[ST2]:
        if (A)
          NextState[ST1] = 1'b1;
        else
          NextState[ST2] = 1'b1;
    endcase
  end
endmodule
// Synthesized netlist is shown in Figure 3-10.
```

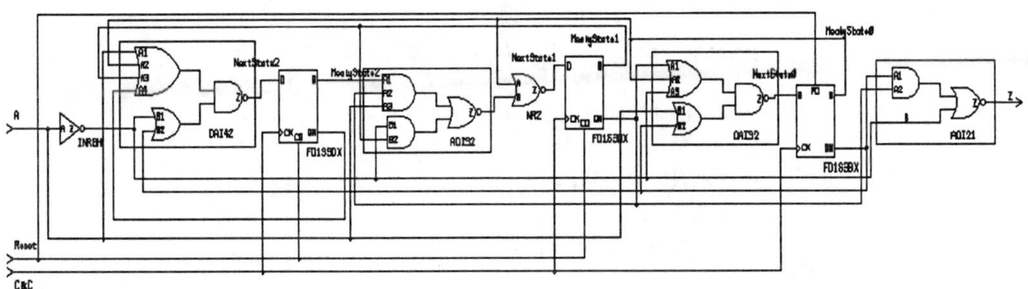

Figure 3-10 One-hot encoding state machine example.

3.5.3 Encoding States

There are many ways to model the machine states of a finite state machine. Described here are some of the most common ones. The

MooreFSM module described earlier is used as an example in describing these encodings.

Using Integers

The simplest way is to assign integer values to states.

```
integer MooreState;
. . .
case (MooreState)
   0 : . . .
    MooreState = 2;
    . . .
   1 :
    . . .
endcase
```

The problem with this approach is that since it is impractical to list all possible values an integer can take, to avoid latches either the default case branch must be specified or the full_case synthesis directive must be used. Another problem with this approach is not good readability.

Using Parameter Declarations

Another option is to declare parameters and use these in the case statement.

```
parameter S0 = 0, S1 = 1, S2 = 2, S3 = 3;

reg [0:1] MooreState;
. . .
case (MooreState)
   S0 : . . .
    MooreState = S2;
    . . .
   S1 :
    . . .
endcase
```

The advantage of this approach is that the state encodings are described explicitly in one place and can be changed easily. If either the parameter declarations or the integer values are used directly, a synthesis system uses the minimum number of bits needed to encode the integer value. In the above example, only two bits are needed for state encoding since the maximum integer value is 3.

What if a different encoding has to be specified? This can be done by describing each state as a vector of bits.

```
parameter S0 = 3'b000, S1 = 3'b001, S2 = 3'b010,
          S3 = 3'100;

reg [0:2] MooreState;
. . .
case (MooreState)
  S0 : . . .
   MooreState = S2;
   . . .
  S1 :
   . . .
endcase
```

In this case, the number of bits required for state encoding is dictated by the number of bits in the parameter which in this example is 3 bits. Of course, the machine state *MooreState* must be made wide enough to hold the new size of three bits.

3.6 Modeling an Universal Shift Register

Here is a synthesis model of a 3-bit universal shift register. The universal shift register performs the following functions:

i. hold value
ii. shift left
iii. shift right
iv. load value

This universal register can be used as a serial-in, serial-out shift register, parallel-in, serial-out shift register, serial-in, parallel-out shift register, and as a parallel-in, parallel-out shift register. Here is the state table for the 3-bit universal shift register.

Function	*Inputs* (*S0 S1*)	*Next state* (*Q*[2]	*Q*[1]	*Q*[0])
Hold	0 0	*Q*[2]	*Q*[1]	*Q*[0]
Shift left	0 1	*Q*[1]	*Q*[0]	*RightIn*
Shift right	1 0	*LeftIn*	*Q*[2]	*Q*[1]
Load	1 1	*ParIn*[2]	*ParIn*[1]	*ParIn*[0]

The synthesis model follows.

```
module UnivShiftRegister (Clock, Clear, LeftIn,
                          RightIn, S0, S1, ParIn, Q);
  input Clock, Clear, LeftIn, RightIn, S0, S1;
  input [2:0] ParIn;
  output [2:0] Q;
  reg [2:0] Q;

  always @(negedge Clear or posedge Clock)
    if (! Clear)
      Q <= 3'b000;
    else
      case ({S0, S1})
        2'b00 : ;
        2'b01 :
          Q <= {Q[1:0], RightIn};
        2'b10 :
          Q <= {LeftIn, Q[2:1]};
        2'b11 :
          Q <= ParIn;
      endcase
endmodule
// Synthesized netlist is shown in Figure 3-11.
```

3.7 Modeling an ALU

3.7.1 A Parameterized ALU

Here is an example of a parameterized *N*-bit arithmetic-logic-unit that performs an exclusive-or, less than, and an increment-by-1 operation.

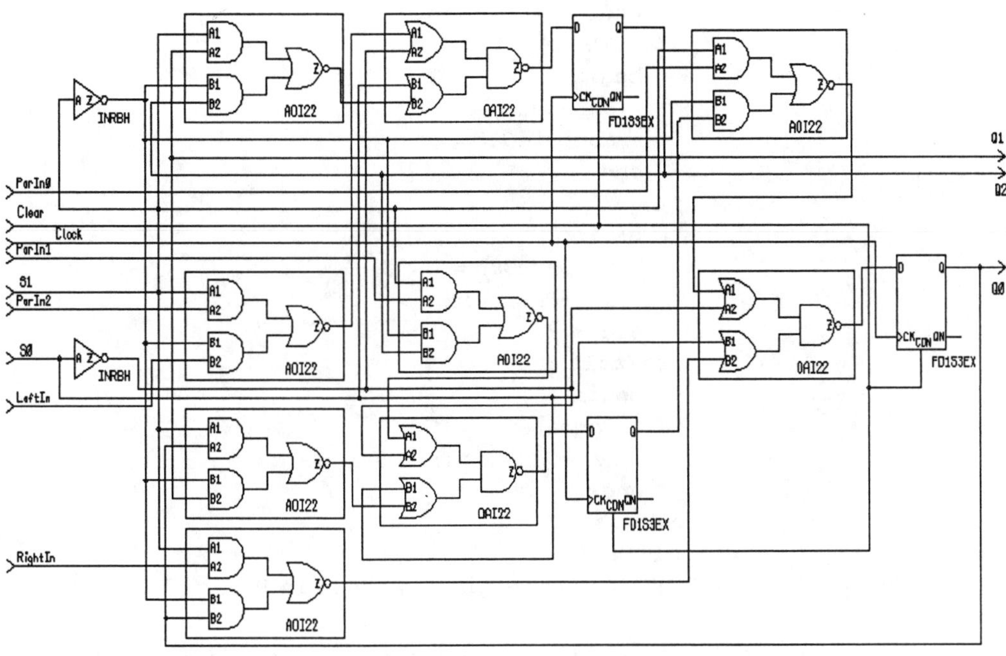

Figure 3-11 A 3-bit universal shift register.

```
module ArithLogicUnit (A, B, Select, CompareOut,
                       DataOut);
  parameter N = 2;
  input [N-1:0] A, B;
  input [2:0] Select;
  output CompareOut;
  output [N-1:0] DataOut;
  reg CompareOut;
  reg [N-1:0] DataOut;

  parameter OP_XOR = 3'b001, OP_INCRA = 3'b010,
            OP_LT = 3'b100;

  always @ (A or B or Select)
    case (Select)
      OP_INCRA :
        begin
          DataOut = A + 1;
```

```
          CompareOut = 'bx;
        end
      OP_XOR :
        begin
          DataOut = A ^ B;
          CompareOut = 'bx;
        end
      OP_LT :
        begin
          CompareOut = A < B;
          DataOut = 'bx;
        end
      default :
        begin
          CompareOut = 'bx;
          DataOut = 'bx;
        end
    endcase
endmodule
// Synthesized netlist is shown in Figure 3-12.
```

A different size ALU can be synthesized by specifying a different value for the parameter when it is instantiated. This is shown in the following example for a 4-bit ALU.

```
module FourBitALU (A, B, Sel, Cmp, Data);
  parameter ALU_SIZE = 4;
  input [ALU_SIZE-1:0] A, B;
  input [2:0] Sel;
  output Cmp;
  output [ALU_SIZE-1:0] Data;

  ArithLogicUnit #(ALU_SIZE) InstA (A, B, Sel,
                                    Cmp, Data);
endmodule
```

3.7.2 A Simple ALU

Here is a model of a different simple arithmetic-logic-unit. This logic unit performs four functions: add, nand, greater-than and exclusive-or. A continuous assignment statement with a conditional expression is used to model the arithmetic-logic-unit.

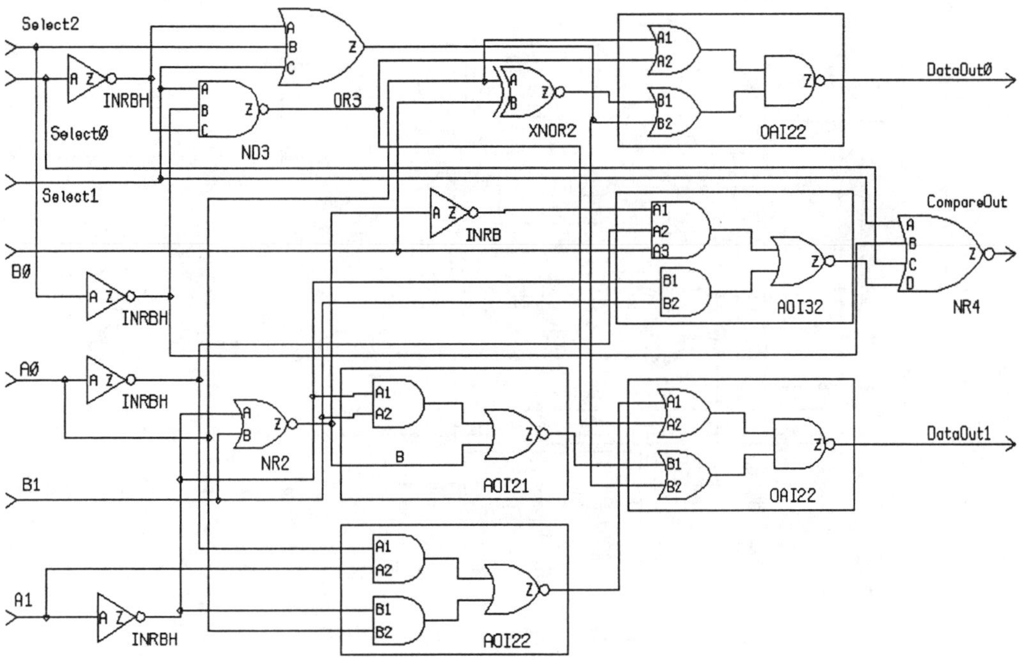

Figure 3-12 A 2-bit ALU.

```
module CustomALU (A, B, OpCode, DataZ, CompZ);
  parameter NBITS = 2;
  input [NBITS-1:0] A, B;
  input [1:0] OpCode;
  output [NBITS-1:0] DataZ;
  output CompZ;
  parameter ADD_OP = 0, NAND_OP = 1, GT_OP = 2,
            XOR_OP = 3;

  assign DataZ = (OpCode == ADD_OP) ? A + B :
                 (OpCode == NAND_OP) ? ~ (A & B) :
                 (OpCode == XOR_OP) ? A ^ B :
                 'bx;

  assign CompZ = (OpCode == GT_OP) ? A > B : 'bx;
endmodule
// Synthesized netlist is shown in Figure 3-13.
```

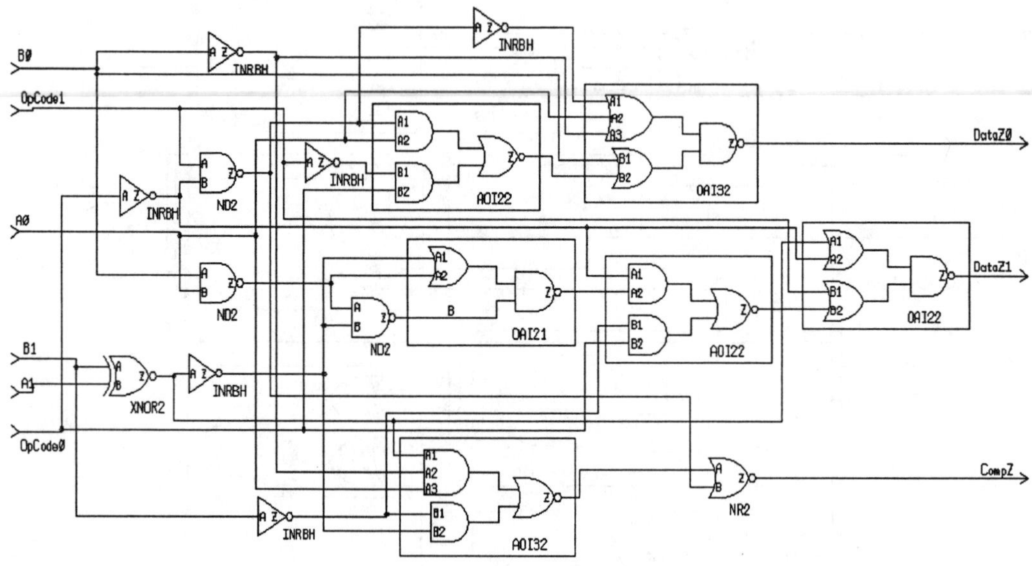

Figure 3-13 A 2-bit custom ALU.

3.8 Modeling a Counter

3.8.1 Binary Counter

Here is a model for a parameterized *N*-bit binary up-down counter with synchronous preset and preclear controls. The counting is synchronized to the rising edge of a clock.

```
module BinaryCounter (Ck, UpDown, PresetClear,
                        LoadData, DataIn, Q, QN);
  parameter NBITS = 2;
  input Ck, UpDown, PresetClear, LoadData;
  input [NBITS-1:0] DataIn;
  output [NBITS-1:0] Q;
  output [NBITS-1:0] QN;

  reg [NBITS-1:0] Counter;
```

```
  always @ (posedge Ck)
    if (PresetClear)
      Counter <= 0;
    else if (~ LoadData)
      Counter <= DataIn;
    else if (UpDown)
      Counter <= Counter + 1;
    else
      Counter <= Counter - 1;

  assign Q = Counter;
  assign QN = ~ Counter;
endmodule
// Synthesized netlist of a 2-bit binary counter is
// shown in Figure 3-14.
```

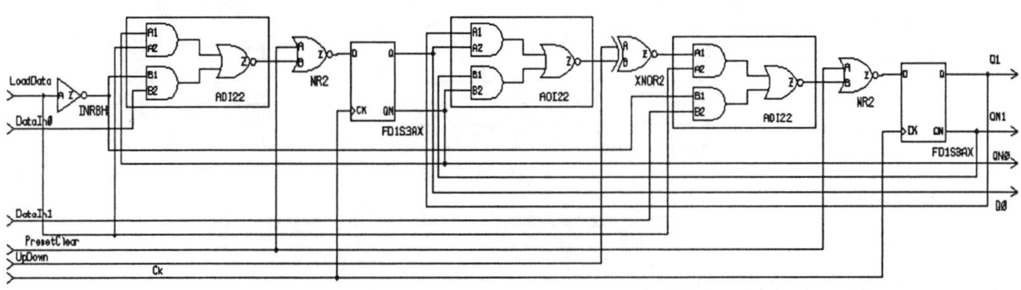

Figure 3-14 A 2-bit up-down, loadable, clearable binary counter.

3.8.2 Modulo-*N* Counter

Here is a model of a modulo-*N* binary up-counter. This counter has only a synchronous preclear control and all transitions occur on the rising clock edge.

```
// Number of bits in counter: NBITS
// Modulo: UPTO
module ModuloN_Cntr (Clock, Clear, Q, QBAR);
  parameter NBITS = 2, UPTO = 3;
  input Clock, Clear;
  output [NBITS-1:0] Q, QBAR;
  reg [NBITS-1:0] Counter;
```

```
    always @ (posedge Clock)
      if (Clear)
        Counter <= 0;
      else
        Counter <= (Counter + 1) % UPTO;

    assign Q = Counter;
    assign QBAR = ~ Counter;
  endmodule
  // Synthesized netlist for a modulo-3 counter is shown
  // in Figure 3-15.
```

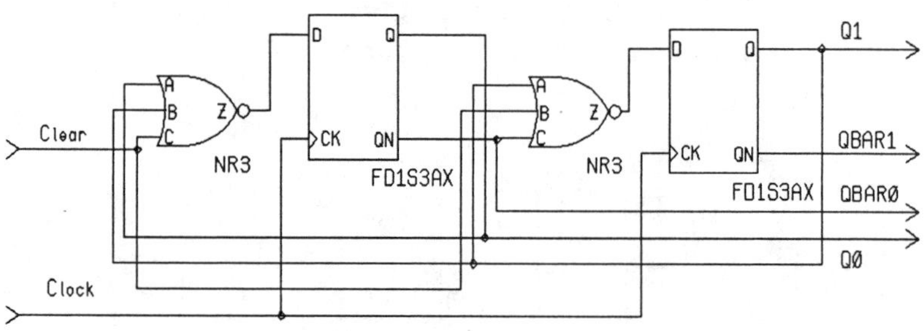

Figure 3-15 A modulo-3 binary counter.

3.8.3 Johnson Counter

A Johnson counter is a shift-type counter. Here is an example of a 3-bit Johnson counter stream.

```
000
001
011
111
110
100
000
```

The keys to modeling a Johnson counter are:

i. If the most significant bit (the leftmost bit) of the counter is a 1, then a 0 has to be shifted in from the right.

ii. If the most significant bit is a 0, then a 1 has to be shifted in from the right.

Here is the model for a parameterized *N*-bit Johnson counter with an asynchronous preclear control.

```
module JohnsonCounter (ClockJ, PreClear, Q);
  parameter NBITS = 3;
  input ClockJ, PreClear;
  output [1:NBITS] Q;
  reg [1:NBITS] Q;

  always @ (negedge PreClear or negedge ClockJ)
    if (! PreClear)
      Q <= 0;
    else
    begin
      if (! Q[1])
        Q <= {Q[2:NBITS], 1'b1};
      else
        Q <= {Q[2:NBITS], 1'b0};
    end
endmodule
// Synthesized netlist for a 3-bit Johnson counter is
// shown in Figure 3-16.
```

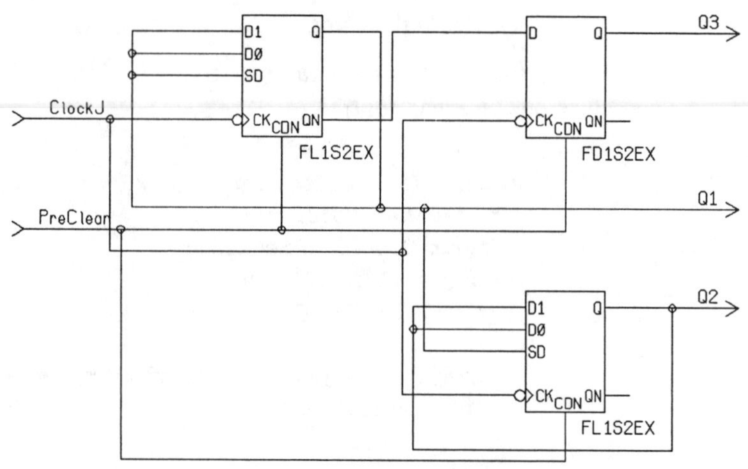

Figure 3-16 A 3-bit Johnson counter.

3.8.4 Gray Counter

A Gray counter is a binary counter with the following conversion logic:

i. The first Gray bit (the leftmost bit) is the same as the first binary bit.

ii. The second Gray bit is determined by xor'ing the second binary bit with the first binary bit, and so on; that is, each pair of adjacent bits are xor'ed to get the next Gray bit.

For example, a binary count of 4'b1100 corresponds to a Gray count of 4'b1010. Here is a Verilog HDL model for a parameterized *N*-bit Gray up-counter with synchronous preclear.

```
module GrayCounter (ClockG, Clear, Q, QN);
  parameter NBITS = 3;
  input ClockG, Clear;
  output [1:NBITS] Q, QN;

  reg [1:NBITS] Counter, GrayCount;
  integer K;

  always @ (posedge ClockG)
```

```
      if (Clear)
        Counter <= 0;
      else
        Counter <= Counter + 1;

    always @ (Counter)
    begin
      GrayCount[1] = Counter[1];

      for (K = 2; K <= NBITS; K = K+1)
        GrayCount[K] = Counter[K-1] ^ Counter[K];
    end

    assign Q = GrayCount;
    assign QN = ~ GrayCount;
  endmodule
  // Synthesized netlist for a 3-bit Gray counter is shown
  // in Figure 3-17.
```

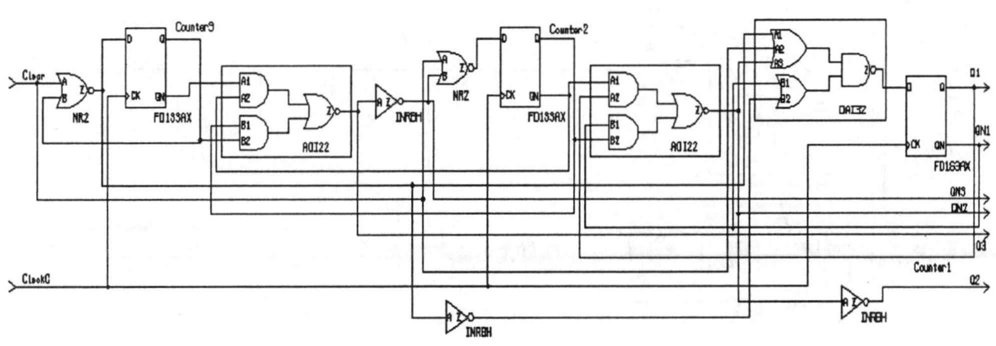

Figure 3-17 A 3-bit Gray counter.

3.9 Modeling a Parameterized Adder

Here is a model for a parameterized *N*-bit adder with carry input and carry output. The leftmost bit is the most significant bit. Figure 3-18 shows the synthesized netlist for a 3-bit adder with carry-in and carry-out.

```
module AddWithCarryInCarryOut (OpdA, OpdB, CarryIn,
                               CarryOut, Sum);
  parameter NUMBITS = 3;
  input [NUMBITS:1] OpdA, OpdB;
  input CarryIn;
  output CarryOut;
  output [NUMBITS:1] Sum;

  assign {CarryOut, Sum} = OpdA + OpdB + CarryIn;
endmodule
// Synthesized netlist for a 3-bit parameterized adder
// is shown in Figure 3-18.
```

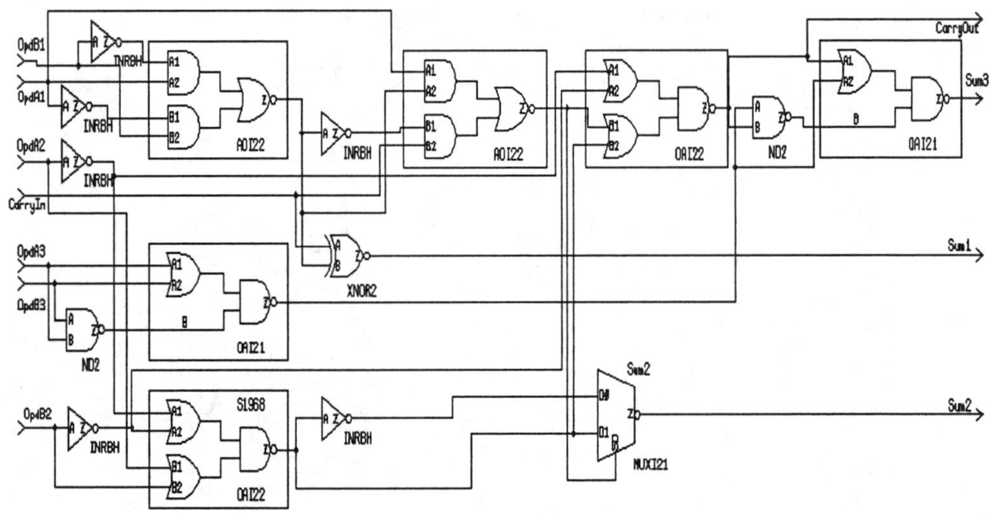

Figure 3-18 A 3-bit adder with carry-in and carry-out.

3.10 Modeling a Parameterized Comparator

Here is a model for a parameterized *N*-bit binary comparator. The input vectors are treated as unsigned quantities and a numerical comparison is made.

```
module Comparator (A, B, EQ, GT, LT, NE, GE, LE);
  parameter NUMBITS = 2;
  input [NUMBITS:1] A, B;
  output EQ, GT, LT, NE, GE, LE;

  reg [5:0] ResultBus;
  // Bit 5 is EQ, bit 4 is GT, 3 is LT, 2 is NE,
  // 1 is GE and 0 is LE.

  always @ (A or B)
    if (A == B)
      ResultBus = 6'b100011;
    else if (A < B)
      ResultBus = 6'b001101;
    else // (A > B)
      ResultBus = 6'b010110;

  assign {EQ, GT, LT, NE, GE, LE} = ResultBus;
endmodule
// Synthesized netlist for a 2-bit comparator is shown
// in Figure 3-19.
```

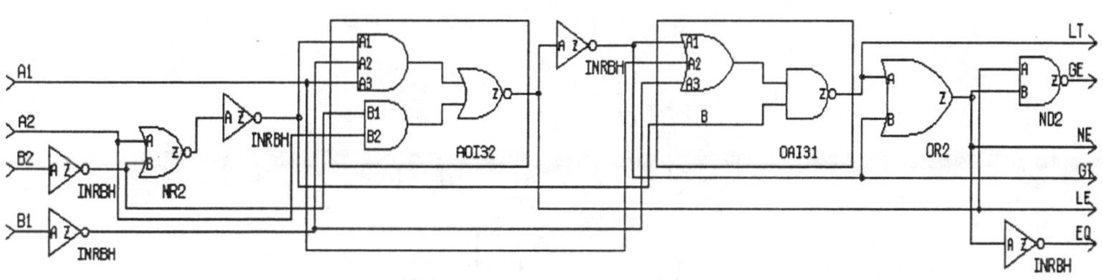

Figure 3-19 A 2-bit comparator.

3.11 Modeling a Decoder

3.11.1 A Simple Decoder

Here is an example of a simple 2-by-4 decoder circuit. This is a combinational circuit modeled purely using continuous assignment statements. Delays specified with the assignment statements, if any, are typically ignored by a synthesis system.

```
module SimpleDecoder (A, B, Enable, DecodeOut);
  input A, B, Enable;
  output [0:3] DecodeOut;
  wire Abar, Bbar;

  assign Abar = ~ A;
  assign Bbar = ~ B;
  assign DecodeOut[0] = ~ (Enable & Abar & Bbar);
  assign DecodeOut[1] = ~ (Enable & Abar & B);
  assign DecodeOut[2] = ~ (Enable & A & Bbar);
  assign DecodeOut[3] = ~ (Enable & A & B);
endmodule
// Synthesized netlist is shown in Figure 3-20.
```

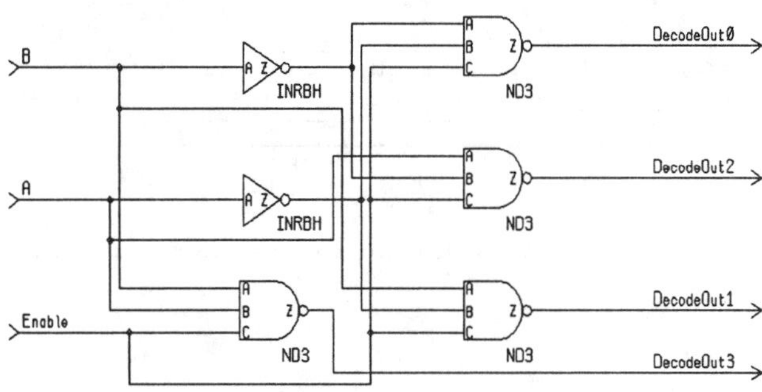

Figure 3-20 A simple 2-by-4 decoder.

3.11.2 Binary Decoder

Here is a model of a parameterized *N*-bit binary decoder.

```
module BinaryDecoder (SelectAddress, DecodeOut);
  parameter SBITS = 2;
  parameter OUT_BITS = 4; // Should be 2 to power of SBITS
  input [SBITS-1:0] SelectAddress;
  output [OUT_BITS-1:0] DecodeOut;
  reg [OUT_BITS-1:0] DecodeOut;

  integer k;

  always @ (SelectAddress)
    for (k = OUT_BITS - 1; k >= 0; k = k - 1)
      DecodeOut[k] = (k == SelectAddress) ? 'b1 : 'b0;
endmodule
// Synthesized netlist of a 2-bit binary decoder is shown
// in Figure 3-21.
```

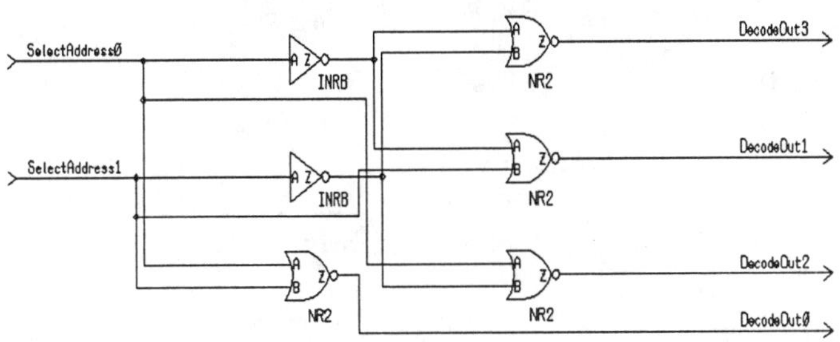

Figure 3-21 A 2-bit binary decoder.

3.11.3 Johnson Decoder

Here is a model of a parameterized *N*-bit Johnson decoder with an enable control.

```
module JohnsonDecoder (S, En, Y);
  parameter N = 3;
  input [0:N-1] S;
  input En;
  output [0:2*N-1] Y;
  reg [0:2*N-1] Y;

  reg [0:2*N-1] Address;
  integer J;
```

```
    always @ (S or En)
      if (En == 'b1)
      begin
        Address = 0;

        for (J = 0; J < N; J = J + 1)
          if (S[J])
            Address = Address + 1;

        if (S[0])
          Address = 2*N - Address;

        Y = 'b0;
        Y[Address] = 'b1;
      end
      else if (En == 'b0)
        Y = 'b0;
      else
        Y = 'bx;
endmodule
// Synthesized netlist for a 3-bit Johnson decoder is
// shown in Figure 3-22.
```

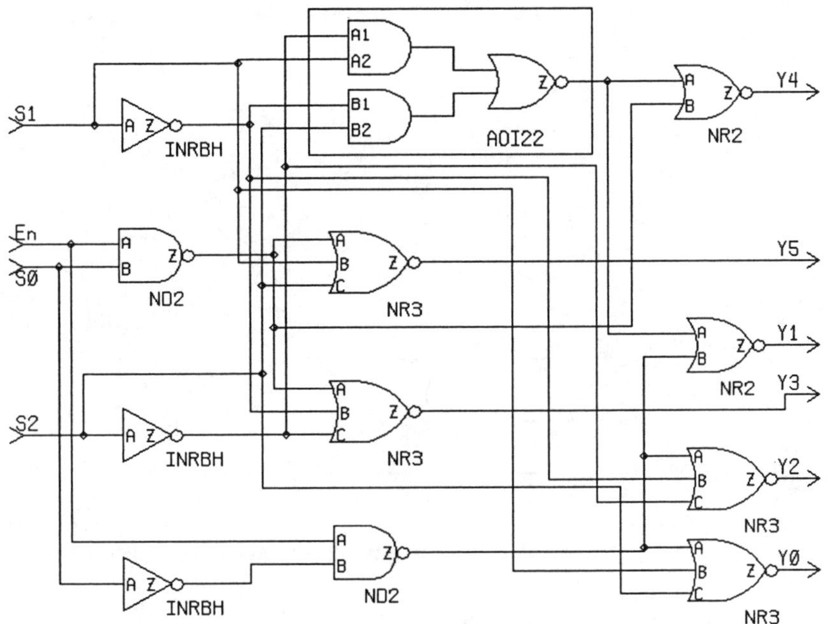

Figure 3-22 A 3-bit Johnson decoder.

3.12 Modeling a Multiplexer

3.12.1 A Simple Multiplexer

Here is a model of a 4-by-1 multiplexer circuit. In this case, a bit-select in a continuous assignment statement has been used to model the combinational logic.

```
module SimpleMultiplexer (DataIn, SelectAddr, MuxOut);
  input [0:3] DataIn;
  input [0:1] SelectAddr;
  output MuxOut;

  assign MuxOut = DataIn[SelectAddr];
```

```
endmodule
// Synthesized netlist is shown in Figure 3-23.
```

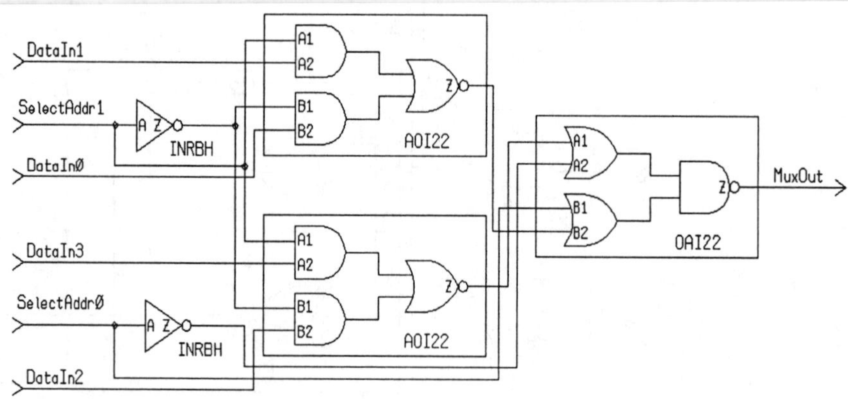

Figure 3-23 A 4-by-1 multiplexer.

3.12.2 A Parameterized Multiplexer

Here is a model of a parameterized multiplexer. The number of bits per word and the number of words in the multiplexer are modeled as parameters. The input data lines are represented as a single array *DataBus*. The multiplexer has select lines which are non-encoded, and an enable signal. Inverted outputs are also provided. All outputs are three-state'ed based on the *Enable* condition.

```
module BinaryMultiplexer (DataBus, Select, Enable,
                          Y, Ybar);
  parameter NBITS = 2, WORDS = 2;
  input [NBITS * WORDS-1:0] DataBus;
    // DataBus is a linearized 2D array.
  input [WORDS-1:0] Select;     // Decoded select lines.
  input Enable;
  output [NBITS-1:0] Y, Ybar;
  reg [NBITS-1:0] Y, Ybar;

  integer K;

  function [WORDS-1:0] GetWordIndex;
```

```
    // Gets the first index that has value 1.
    input [WORDS-1:0] DecodedSelect;
    integer Inx;
    begin
      GetWordIndex = 0;

      for (Inx = WORDS - 1; Inx >= 0; Inx = Inx - 1)
        if (DecodedSelect[Inx] == 'b1)
          GetWordIndex = Inx;
    end
  endfunction

  always @ (DataBus or Select or Enable)
    if (Enable == 'b1)
    begin
      for (K = 0; K < NBITS; K = K + 1)
        Y[K] = DataBus[GetWordIndex(Select) * NBITS
                       + K];

      Ybar = ~ Y;
    end
    else if (Enable == 'b0)
    begin
      Y = 'bz;
      Ybar = 'bz;
    end
    else
    begin
      Y = 'bx;
      Ybar = 'bx;
    end
endmodule
// Synthesized netlist of a 2-by-2 multiplexer is shown
// in Figure 3-24.
```

3.13 Modeling a Parameterized Parity Generator

Here is a model of a parameterized *N*-bit parity generator circuit. The model provides both an odd parity and an even parity output.

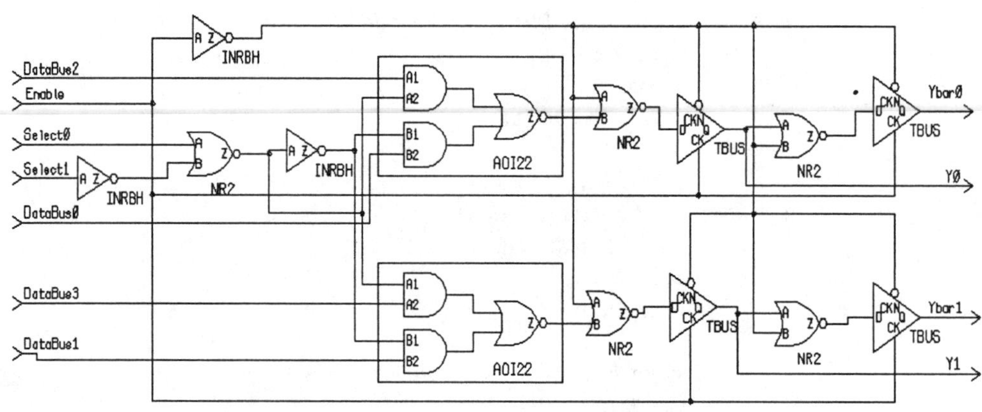

Figure 3-24 A 2-by-2 binary multiplexer.

```
module ParityGenerator (DataIn, OddPar, EvenPar);
  parameter NBITS = 4;
  input [NBITS-1:0] DataIn;
  output OddPar, EvenPar;

  assign EvenPar = ^ DataIn;
  assign OddPar = ~ EvenPar;
endmodule
// Synthesized netlist of a 4-bit parity generator is
// shown in Figure 3-25.
```

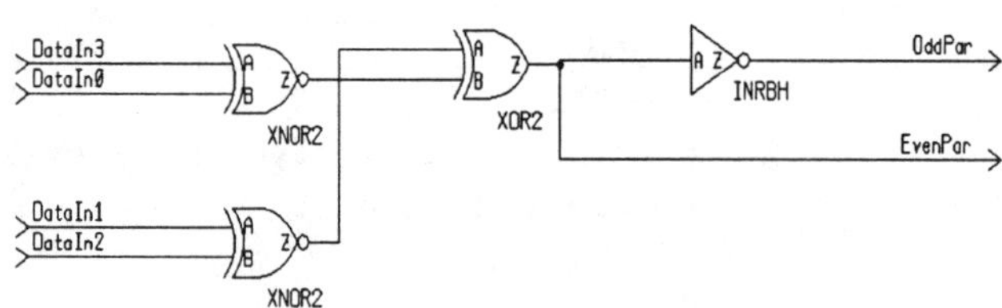

Figure 3-25 A 4-bit parity generator.

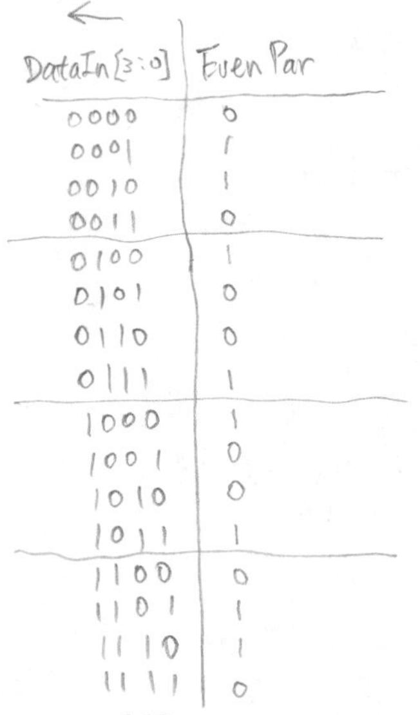

DataIn[3:0]	Even Par
0000	0
0001	1
0010	1
0011	0
0100	1
0101	0
0110	0
0111	1
1000	1
1001	0
1010	0
1011	1
1100	0
1101	1
1110	1
1111	0

3.14 Modeling a Three-state Gate

A three-state gate is modeled by assigning the value z to a variable under the control of a condition. Here is an example.

```
module ThreeStateGates (ReadState, CpuBus, MainBus);
  input ReadState;
  input [0:3] CpuBus;
  output [0:3] MainBus;
  reg [0:3] MainBus;

  always @ (ReadState or CpuBus)
    if (ReadState)
      MainBus = 4'bz;
    else
      MainBus = CpuBus;
endmodule
// Synthesized netlist is shown in Figure 3-26.
```

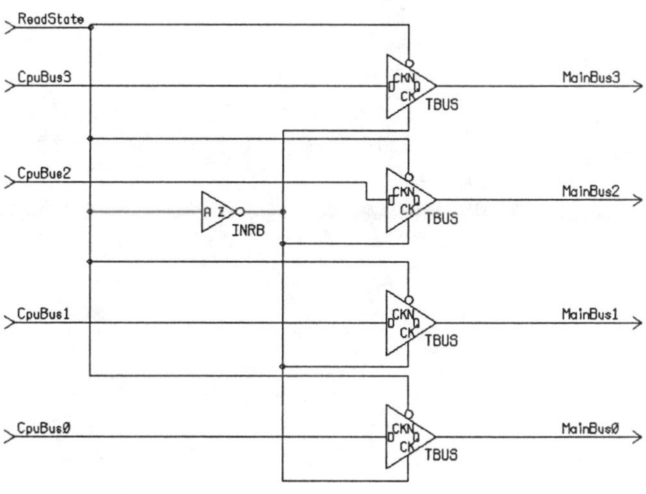

Figure 3-26 A bank of three-state gates.

The variable *MainBus* is three-state'ed as long as *ReadState* is true. If *ReadState* is false, the value of *CpuBus* is assigned to *MainBus*.

3.15 A Count Three 1's Model

Here is a model that detects three 1's in a data stream appearing on input *Data*. The input is checked on every falling edge of clock. If three consecutive 1's are found on the input, the output is set to true, else it is set to false.

```
module Count3Ones (Data, Clock, Reset, SeqFound);
  input Data, Clock, Reset;
  output SeqFound;
  reg SeqFound;

  parameter PATTERN_SEARCHED_FOR = 3'b111;
  reg [2:0] Previous;

  always @ (negedge Clock)
    if (Reset)
    begin
      Previous <= 3'b000;
      SeqFound <= 1'b0;
    end
    else
    begin
      Previous <= {Previous[1:0], Data};
      SeqFound <= (Previous == PATTERN_SEARCHED_FOR);
    end
endmodule
// Synthesized netlist is shown in Figure 3-27.
```

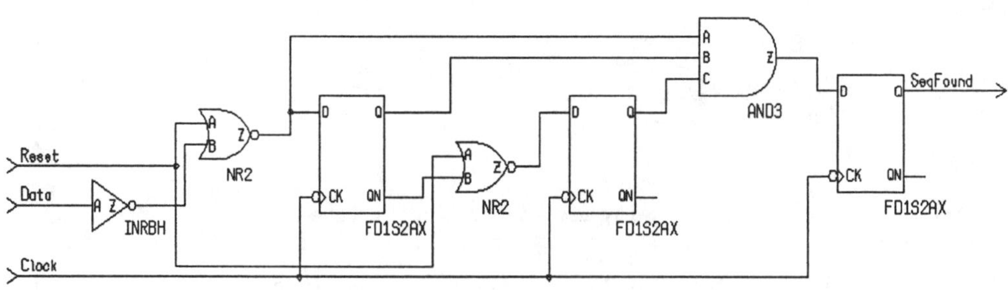

Figure 3-27 Circuit counts three consecutive ones.

Synthesis infers four flip-flops for this model, three for variable *Previous* and one for *SeqFound*. However, optimization reveals that one of the flip-flops for *Previous* is not necessary and hence it is removed. In this model, the output is latched since it is assigned a value under the control of a clock edge. If a latched output is not desired, then the assignment to *SeqFound* must be done outside the always statement. Such a module is shown next.

```
module NoLatchedOutput (Data, Clock, Reset, SeqFound);
  input Data, Clock, Reset;
  output SeqFound;

  parameter PATTERN_SEARCHED_FOR = 3'b111;
  reg [2:0] Previous;

  always @ (negedge Clock)
    if (Reset)
      Previous <= 3'b000;
    else
      Previous <= {Previous[1:0], Data};

  assign SeqFound = (Previous == PATTERN_SEARCHED_FOR);
endmodule
// Synthesized netlist is shown in Figure 3-28.
```

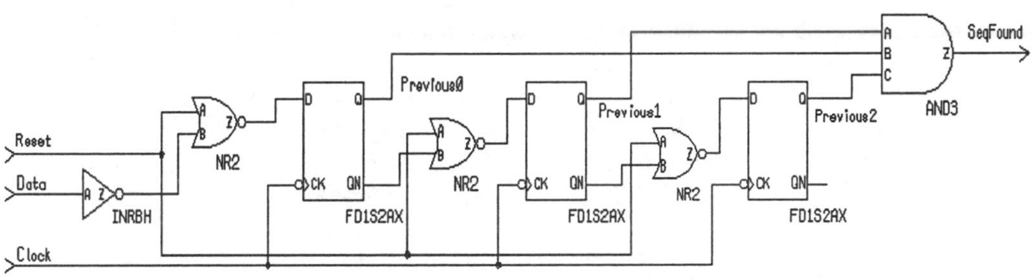

Figure 3-28 No latched output.

In this module, the output *SeqFound* is not latched. Synthesis infers three flip-flops for variable *Previous*; note that in this case, all the bits of *Previous* have to be latched.

3.16 A Factorial Model

Here is a model that generates the factorial of a number given in *Data*. The result is output in *Result* and *Exponent* as mantissa and exponent respectively. The exponent is base 2. The input *Reset* causes the model to reset.

```
module Factorial (Reset, Start, Clk, Data, Done,
                  Result, Exponent);
  input Reset, Start, Clk;
  input [4:0] Data;
  output Done;                    // Acknowledge signal.
  reg Done;
  output [7:0] Result, Exponent;
  reg [7:0] Result, Exponent;

  reg [4:0] InLatch;

  always @ (posedge Clk)
  begin: BLOCK_A
    integer NextResult, J;

    if ((Start && Done) || Reset)
    begin
      Result <= 'b1;
      Exponent <= 'b0;
      InLatch <= Data;
      Done <= 'b0;
    end
    else
    begin
      if ((InLatch > 1) && (! Done))
      begin
        NextResult = Result * InLatch;
        InLatch <= InLatch - 1;
      end
      else
        NextResult = Result;

      if (InLatch <= 1)
        Done <= 'b1;
```

```
        for (J = 1; J <= 5; J = J + 1)
        begin
          if (NextResult > 256)
          begin
            NextResult = NextResult >> 1;
            Exponent <= Exponent + 1;
          end
        end

        Result <= NextResult;
      end
    end
  endmodule
```

When synthesized, flip-flops are inferred for *InLatch*, *Result*, *Exponent* and *Done*.

3.17 An UART Model

Here is a model of a synthesizable UART circuit. This circuit converts RS-232 serial input data into parallel data out, and the parallel input data into RS-232 serial data out. The data byte is 8 bits in length. There are four major blocks in this UART model, as shown in Figure 3-29: *RX*, the receiver block, *TX*, the transmitter block, *DIV*, the clock divider and *MP*, the microprocessor block.

The first block *DIV* is a frequency divider. This block has 2 modes of operation, the normal mode and the test mode. In the test mode, the UART chip runs 16 times faster than in the normal mode. Also, the transmission data rate of the UART chip is 16 times faster than the receiving rate. Each block is initialized by setting the reset line low by applying a 0 to port *MR*. The *TX* block accepts 8-bit parallel data from the microprocessor interface (*MP*) block and transmits it serially to the RS-232 port through port *DOUT*. Conversely, the *RX* block receives serial data input, and sends it in 8-bit parallel format to the *MP* block. Again, the transmitter runs at 16 times the speed of the receiver. The microprocessor interface (*MP*) block asynchronously controls the parallel data flow between the *RX* / *TX* blocks and the microprocessor data bus.

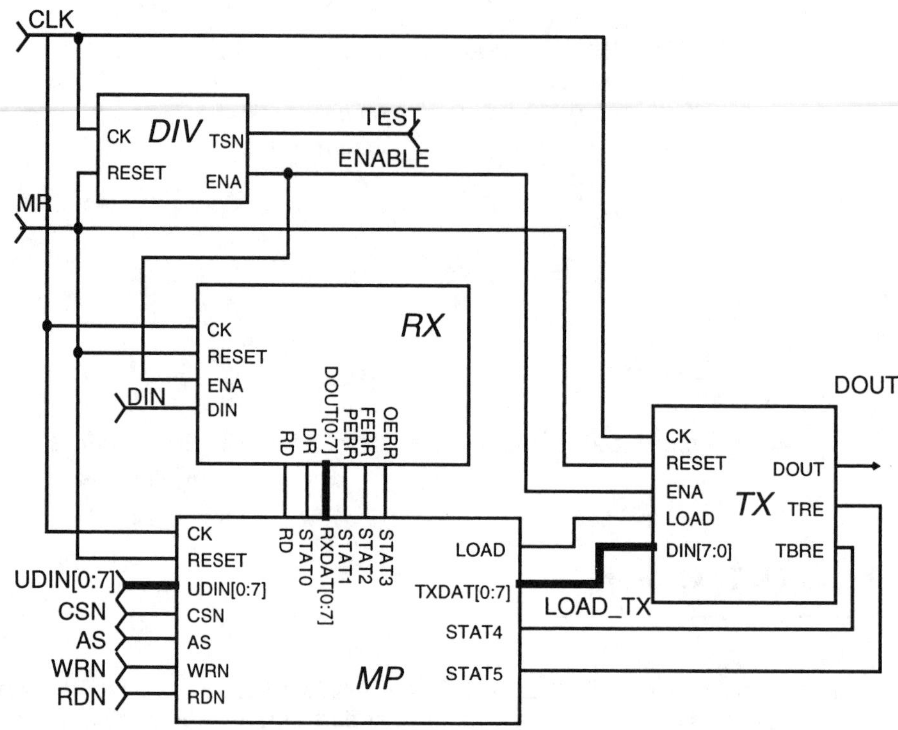

Figure 3-29 The UART circuit.

The *UART* top-level model glues all these blocks together using module instantiations. The microprocessor entity, *MP*, is described in the structural style, that is, using module instances. The remaining three are described using the behavioral style. In this chapter, only the behavioral blocks are described.

Here is the behavioral model for the transmitter block *TX*. This model is a synthesizable model. Rising-edge-triggered flip-flops are inferred for variables *TBR*, *TR*, *TRE*, *TBRE*, *DOUT*, *CBIT* and *PA*; this is because these variables are assigned values under the control of clock *CK*.

```
module TX (CK, RESET, ENABLE, TLOAD, DIN, DOUT,
           TRE, TBRE);
  input CK, RESET, ENABLE, TLOAD;
  input [7:0] DIN;
  output DOUT, TRE, TBRE;
```

```
reg DOUT, TRE, TBRE;

reg [7:0] TBR, TR;
reg [3:0] CBIT;
reg PA;

always @ (posedge CK)
begin
  if (! RESET)
  begin
    TRE <= 'b1;
    TBRE <= 'b1;
    DOUT <= 'b1;
    CBIT <= 4'b0;
    PA <= 'b0;
  end
  else if (TLOAD)
  begin
    TBR <= DIN;
    TBRE <= 'b0;
  end
  else if (ENABLE)
  begin
    if (! TBRE && TRE)
    begin
      TR <= TBR;
      TRE <= 'b0;
      TBRE <= 'b1;
    end

    if (! TRE)
      case (CBIT)
        4'b0000:
          begin
            DOUT <= 'b0;
            CBIT <= CBIT + 1;
          end
        4'b0001, 4'b0010, 4'b0011, 4'b0100,
        4'b0101, 4'b0110, 4'b0111, 4'b1000:
          begin
            DOUT <= TR[0];
            PA <= PA ^ TR[0];
            TR <= {1'b1, TR[7:1]};
```

```
          CBIT <= CBIT + 1;
        end
      4'b1001:
        begin
          DOUT <= PA;
          PA <= 'b0;
          TR <= {1'b1, TR[7:1]};
          CBIT <= CBIT + 1;
        end
      4'b1010:
        begin
          DOUT <= TR[0];
          TR <= {1'b1, TR[7:1]};
          CBIT <= CBIT + 1;
        end
      4'b1011:
        begin
          DOUT <= TR[0];
          TRE <= 1'b1;
          TR <= {1'b1, TR[7:1]};
          CBIT <= 4'b0000;
        end
    endcase
  end              // if (ENABLE)
end                // @(posedge CK)
endmodule
```

Here is the behavioral model for the receiver block *RX*. This model is also synthesizable. Flip-flops are inferred for variables *START*, *CBIT*, *CSAM*, *DI*, *PI*, *SR*, *DR*, *DOUT*, *PERR*, *FERR* and *OERR*.

```
module RX (CK, RESET, ENA, DIN, RD, DR, DOUT,
           PERR, FERR, OERR);
  input CK, RESET, ENA, DIN, RD;
  output DR;
  reg DR;
  output [7:0] DOUT;
  reg [7:0] DOUT;
  output PERR, FERR, OERR;
  reg PERR, FERR, OERR, START;

  reg [3:0] CBIT, CSAM;
```

```
reg DI, PI;
reg [7:0] SR;

always @ (posedge CK)
begin
  if (! RESET)
  begin
    CBIT <= 0;
    CSAM <= 0;
    START <= 0;
    PI <= 0;
    DR <= 0;
    PERR <= 0;
    FERR <= 0;
    OERR <= 0;
  end
  else                                    // if (RESET)
  begin
    if (RD)
      DR <= 0;

    if (ENA)
      if (! START)
      begin
        if (! DIN)
        begin
          CSAM <= CSAM + 1;
          START <= 1;
        end
      end
      else if (CSAM == 8)
      begin
        DI <= DIN;
        CSAM <= CSAM + 1;
      end
      else if (CSAM == 15)
        case (CBIT)
          0:
            begin
              if (DI == 1)
                START <= 0;
              else
                CBIT <= CBIT + 1;
```

```
            CSAM <= CSAM + 1;
          end
        1, 2, 3, 4, 5, 6, 7, 8:
          begin
            CBIT <= CBIT + 1;
            CSAM <= CSAM + 1;
            PI <= PI ^ DI;
            SR  <= {DI, SR[7:1]};
          end
        9:
          begin
            CBIT <= CBIT + 1;
            CSAM <= CSAM + 1;
            PI <= PI ^ DI;
          end
        10:
          begin
            PERR <= PI;
            PI <= 0;

            if ( ! DI)
              FERR <= 1;
            else
              FERR <= 0;

            if (DR)
              OERR <= 1;
            else
              OERR <= 0;

            DR <= 1;
            DOUT <= SR;
            CBIT <= 0;
            START <= 0;
          end
      endcase
      else // ((0 <= CSAM < 8) || (8 < CSAM < 15))
        CSAM <= CSAM + 1;
    end               // if (! RESET)
  end                 // @(posedge CK)
endmodule
```

Here is a synthesizable model for the divider block *DIV*. This circuit produces a pulse every sixteen clock cycles. If input *TESTN* is 0, *ENA* is set to a 1. Variable *COUNT* is inferred as flip-flops.

```
module DIV (CK, RESET, TESTN, ENA);
  input CK, RESET, TESTN;
  output ENA;

  reg [3:0] COUNT;

  always @(posedge CK)
    if (! RESET)
      COUNT <= 0;
    else if (! TESTN)
      COUNT <= 4'hF;
    else
      COUNT <= COUNT + 1;        // Increment counter.

  // Combinational part:
  assign ENA = (COUNT == 15);
endmodule
```

3.18 A Blackjack Model

Here is a synthesizable model of a blackjack program. This program is played with a deck of cards. Cards 2 to 10 have values equal to their face value, and an ace has a value of either 1 or 11. The object of the game is to accept a number of random cards such that the total score (sum of values of all cards) is as close as possible to 21 without exceeding 21.

The input *InsertCard* indicates when the program is ready to accept a new card. A card is accepted at the rising edge of *Clock* if *InsertCard* is true. Input *CardValue* has the value of the card. If a sequence of cards is accepted such that the total falls between 17 and 21, then output *Won* is set to true, indicating that the game has been won. If total exceeds 21, then the program checks to see if an ace was accepted as a 1 or a 11; if it was accepted as a 11, the value of ace is changed to 1 and the program gets ready to accept a new card; if not, output *Lost* is set to true indicating that it has lost. If either *Won* or *Lost* is set, no more cards are accepted. The game can be reset by setting *NewGame* to true.

```
module Blackjack (CardValue, Clock, InsertCard,
                  NewGame, TotalPoints, Won, Lost);
  input [0:3] CardValue;
  input Clock, InsertCard, NewGame;
  output [0:5] TotalPoints;
  output Won, Lost;
  reg Won, Lost;

  reg AceAvailable, AceValueIs11;
  reg [0:5] TotPts;
  parameter TRUE = 1'b1, FALSE = 1'b0;

  always @ (posedge NewGame or posedge Clock)
    if (NewGame)
    begin
      Won <= FALSE;
      Lost <= FALSE;
      AceAvailable = FALSE;
      AceValueIs11 = FALSE;
      TotPts = 0;
    end
    else        // posedge Clock
      if (InsertCard && ! Won && ! Lost)
      begin
        if (CardValue == 4'd11)
        begin
          AceAvailable = TRUE;
          AceValueIs11 = TRUE;
        end

        TotPts = TotPts + CardValue;

        if ((TotPts >= 17) && (TotPts <= 21))
          Won <= TRUE;
        else if ((TotPts >= 22) && (TotPts <= 31))
        begin
          if (AceAvailable && AceValueIs11)
          begin
            AceValueIs11 = FALSE;
            TotPts = TotPts - 10;
          end
          else
            Lost <= TRUE;
```

```
      end
    end

  assign TotalPoints = TotPts;
endmodule
```

❑

CHAPTER

4

MODEL OPTIMIZATIONS

This chapter describes optimizations that can be performed on a Verilog HDL model to improve the circuit performance. In a C programming language compiler, an optimizer produces optimized machine code: code is rearranged, moved around, and so on, to reduce the C code execution time. Such optimizations may also be performed by a logic optimizer. Also in synthesis, the logic generated is very sensitive to the way a model is described. Moving a statement from one place to another or splitting up expressions may have a profound impact on the generated logic; it might increase or decrease the number of synthesized gates and change its timing characteristics.

Figure 4-1 shows that different endpoints for best area and best speed are reached by a logic optimizer depending on the starting point provided by a netlist synthesized from Verilog HDL. The various starting points are obtained by rewriting the same Verilog HDL model using different constructs. Unfortunately, no algorithms are yet known that determine what coding style or optimizations produce the desired balance between area and delay.

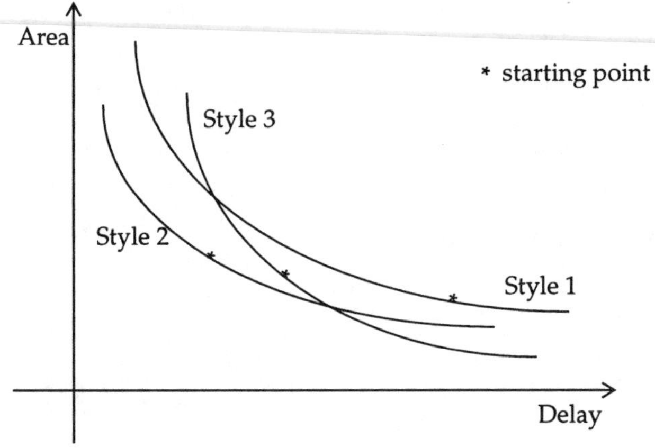

Figure 4-1 Different writing styles produce different area-delay trade-off.

This chapter explores some of these optimizations that may be performed by a designer by rewriting appropriate code in the Verilog HDL synthesis model. These optimizations provide a way to reduce the number of arithmetic and relational operators in the design yielding better quality designs. Synthesis run-times may also be reduced.

4.1 Resource Allocation

Resource allocation refers to the process of sharing an arithmetic-logic-unit (ALU) under mutually-exclusive conditions. Consider the following `if` statement.

```
if (MAX > 100)
  JMA = SMA + BMA;
else
  JMA = SMA - CMA;
```

If no resource allocation is performed, the "+" and "–" operators get synthesized into two separate ALUs. However, if resource allocation is performed, only one ALU is necessary that performs both the "+" and "–" operations. This is because the two operators are used under mutually-exclusive conditions. A multiplexer is also generated; it is needed at the second input port of the ALU to direct inputs *BMA* and *CMA*. Figure 4-2 shows the hardware synthesized for the `if` statement when no resource allocation is performed. Figure 4-3 shows the same example when resource allocation is performed.

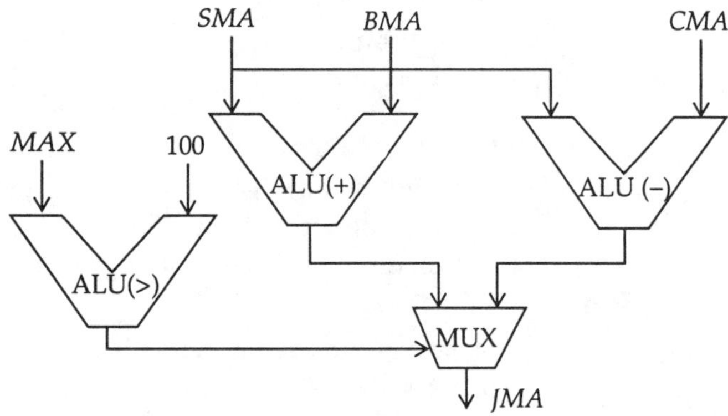

Figure 4-2 Without resource allocation.

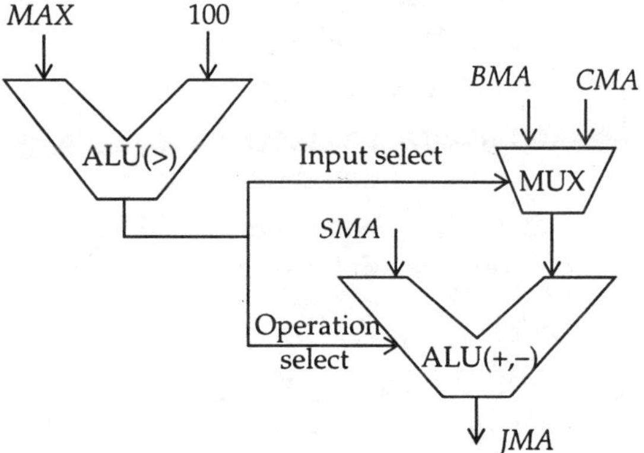

Figure 4-3 With resource allocation.

Notice that with sharing an ALU, a multiplexer has been introduced at one of the inputs of the ALU that contributes to the path delay. However, the amount of logic generated has been reduced due to sharing of the ALU. This is again a trade-off that a designer may have to make, if such a capability is not provided by the synthesis tool. In timing-critical designs, it may be better if no resource sharing is performed.

There are other variations of sharing that a synthesis tool may automatically enforce. Operators that are usually shared are:

i. relational operators

ii. addition

iii. subtraction

iv. multiplication

v. division

Usually it is not worthwhile to generate an ALU that does an addition and a multiplication. Multiplication and division operators are typically shared amongst themselves. When sharing with other operators, the following possibilities exist:

i. Same operator, same operands: definitely must share. Example: $A + B, A + B$

ii. Same operator, one different operand: trade-off, since one multiplexer will be introduced. Example: $A + B, A + C$

iii. Same operator, different operands: trade-off since two multiplexers are introduced. Example: $A + B, C + D$

iv. Different operators, same operands: useful to share. Example: $A + B, A - B$

v. Different operators, one different operand: trade-off since one multiplexer introduced. Example: $A + B, A - C$

vi. Different operators, different operands: trade-off since two multiplexers introduced. Example: $A + B, C - D$

Possibility (*i*) is the best case to share followed by (*iv*), (*ii*, *v*) and (*iii*, *vi*).

Resource allocation may also be performed manually by rewriting the model. Here is such an example.

```
if (! ShReg)
  DataOut = AddrLoad + ChipSelectN;
else if (ReadWrite)
  DataOut = ReadN + WriteN;
```

```
else
  DataOut = AddrLoad + ReadN;

// After manual resource allocation:
if (! ShReg)
begin
  Temp1 = AddrLoad;
  Temp2 = ChipSelectN;
end
else if (ReadWrite)
begin
  Temp1 = ReadN;
  Temp2 = WriteN;
end
else
begin
  Temp1 = AddrLoad;
  Temp2 = ReadN;
end

DataOut = Temp1 + Temp2;
```

The modified model guarantees only one adder and the multiplexers at the input ports of the adder are implied by the `if` statement. The original example may synthesize with three adders.

4.2 Common Subexpressions

It is often useful in practice to identify common subexpressions and to reuse computed values where possible. Here is a simple example.

```
Run = R1 + R2;
. . .
Car = R3 - (R1 + R2);
// Assume that the second assignment is executed every
// time the first statement is executed. Note that this
// assumption may not be true if either of the statements
// is inside an if statement or a case statement.
```

If a synthesis tool does not identify common subexpressions, two adders would be generated, each computing the same result, that of *R1* + *R2*. A logic optimization tool may or may not be able to identify such common logic, thus leading to larger designs. Therefore it is useful to identify common subexpressions and to reuse the computed values. For the previous example, we could replace the second assignment by:

```
Car = R3 - Run;
```

The problem of identifying common subexpressions becomes more important if larger blocks such as multipliers are used.

4.3 Moving Code

It may so happen that within a for-loop statement, there is an expression whose value does not change through every iteration of the loop. Also typically a synthesis tool handles a for-loop by unrolling the loop the specified number of times. In such a case, redundant code is introduced for the expression whose value is invariant of the loop index. Again a logic optimizer may or may not be smart enough to optimize such logic. Performing the optimizations at a higher level, that is, within the model, would help the optimizer in working on more critical pieces of the code. Here is an example of such a for-loop.

```
Car = . . .
. . .
for (Count = 1; Count <= 5; Count = Count + 1)
begin
  . . .
  Tip = Car - 6;
  // Assumption: Car is not assigned a new value within
  // the loop.
  . . .
end
```

The right-hand-side expression in the assignment statement is invariant of the loop index, that is, the value computed in variable *Tip* is independent of the loop index *Count*. However, a synthesis tool may generate five subtracters, one for each loop iteration, thus generating extra logic. In this case, only one subtracter is really necessary.

The best way to handle this case is to move the loop-invariant expression out of the loop. This also improves simulation efficiency. This is shown in the following example.

```
Car = . . .
. . .
Temp = Car - 6;     // A temporary variable is introduced.

for (Count = 1; Count <= 5; Count = Count + 1)
begin
  . . .
  Tip = Temp;
  // Assumption: Car is not assigned a new value within
  // the loop.
  . . .
end
```

Such movement of code should be performed by the designer to produce more efficient code; this gives the logic optimizer a better starting point to begin optimizations.

4.4 Common Factoring

Common factoring is the extraction of common subexpressions in mutually-exclusive branches of an `if` statement or a case statement. Here is an example.

```
if (Test)
  Ax = A & (B + C);
else
  By = (B + C) | T;
```

The expression "*B+C*" is computed in mutually-exclusive branches of an `if` statement. However, instead of the synthesis tool generating two adders, it is useful to factor out the expression and place it before the `if` statement. This is shown next.

```
Temp = B + C;        // A temporary variable is introduced.

if (Test)
  Ax = A & Temp;
else
  By = Temp | T;
```

By performing this common factoring, less logic is synthesized (in the above example, only one adder gets synthesized), a logic optimizer can now concentrate on optimizing more critical areas.

4.5 Commutativity and Associativity

In certain cases, it may be necessary to perform commutative operations before performing some of the earlier mentioned optimizations. Here is an example where performing a commutative operation before common subexpression identification helps in identifying common subexpressions.

```
Run = R1 + R2;
. . .
Car = R3 - (R2 + R1);
```

Applying commutativity rules to the expression "*R2* + *R1*" helps in identifying the common subexpression "*R1* + *R2*" that is also used in the first assignment.

Similarly, associativity rules can be applied before using any of the earlier described optimizations. Here is an example.

```
Lam = A + B + C;
. . .
Bam = C + A - B;
```

Notice that applying associativity and commutativity rules on the expression in the first statement identifies "*C* + *A*" as a common subexpression. After subexpression identification, the example appears like this.

```
Temp = C + A;      // A temporary variable is introduced.
Lam = Temp + B;
Bam = Temp - B;
```

If associativity and commutativity are not used, a synthesis tool may generate three adders and one subtracter; after subexpression identification, it may generate only two adders and one subtracter, thus providing increased savings in logic.

4.6 Other Optimizations

In general, there are two other optimizations that a synthesis tool has no problem handling. These are:

i. Dead-code elimination

ii. Constant folding

These optimizations are usually performed by a synthesis system and a designer does not have to worry about it. These optimizations are nonetheless explained below.

Dead code elimination deletes code that never gets executed. For example,

```
if (2 > 4)
  Oly = Sdy & Rdy;
```

Clearly, there is no need to synthesize an and gate since the assignment statement will never get executed and represents dead code.

Constant folding implies the computation of constant expressions during compile time as opposed to implementing logic and then allowing a logic optimizer to eliminate the logic. Here is a simple example.

```
parameter FAC = 4;
. . .
Yak = 2 * FAC;
```

Constant folding computes the value of the right-hand-side expression during compile time and assigns the value to *Yak*. No hardware need be generated. This leads to savings in logic optimization time.

4.7 Flip-flop and Latch Optimizations

4.7.1 Avoiding Flip-flops

It is important to understand the flip-flop inference rules of a synthesis tool. These rules may vary from one synthesis tool to another. If the inference rules are not followed, a synthesized netlist may have many more flip-flops than are really necessary. Here is a case in point.

```
reg PresentState;
reg [0:3] Zout;
wire ClockA;
. . .
always @ (posedge ClockA)
  case (PresentState)
    0 :
      begin
        PresentState <= 1;
        Zout <= 4'b0100;
      end
    1 :
      begin
        PresentState <= 0;
        Zout <= 4'b0001;
      end
  endcase
```

Here the intention appears to be to store the value of *PresentState* in a flip-flop (rising-edge-triggered). After synthesis, not only is there a flip-flop for *PresentState*, there are also four flip-flops for *Zout*. This is because *Zout* is assigned under the control of a clock. It may or may not be the intention to generate flip-flops for *Zout*. If not, then a case statement needs to be written in a separate always statement in which *Zout* is assigned, this time not under the control of the clock. The modified example that generates only one flip-flop is shown next.

```
always @ (posedge ClockA)          // Flip-flop inference.
  case (PresentState)
    0 : PresentState <= 1;
    1 : PresentState <= 0;
  endcase

always @ (PresentState)            // Combinational logic.
  case (PresentState)
    0 : Zout = 4'b0100;
    1 : Zout = 4'b0001;
  endcase
```

4.7.2 Avoiding Latches

A variable that does not have a value assigned in all branches of a case statement or an `if` statement can lead to a latch being built. This is because in Verilog HDL, a reg variable (assigned within an always statement) infers memory, and thus if the variable is not assigned a value in all branches of a conditional statement, the value needs to be saved in memory. Here is an example.

```
reg Luck;

always @ (Probe or Count)
  if (Probe)
    Luck = Count;
```

What is the value of *Luck* when *Probe* is 0? It must be the old value of *Luck*. Thus the value of *Luck* needs to be saved; a latch is created for this variable.

The best way to avoid latches is to first determine from the synthesis tool how many latches have been inferred. A designer now needs to go back and check if each latch inferred really needs to be a latch. It could be that the designer never intended for a latch or the designer forgot to specify values under all conditions. The best rule is to check the latches that get synthesized and go back and determine why each latch got synthesized and fix code if necessary to avoid any unwanted latches.

Here are two ways of avoiding a latch for the above example. In the first approach, assign a value to the variable in the `else` branch as well.

```
always @ (Probe or Count)
  if (Probe)
    Luck = Count;
    else                    // Else clause added.
      Luck = 0;
```

In the second approach, initialize the value of the variable before the `if` statement.

```
always @ (Probe or Count)
begin
  Luck = 0;   // Value of variable is explicitly
              // initialized.
  if (Probe)
    Luck = Count;
end
```

4.8 Design Size

Small Designs Synthesize Faster

Experimental studies have shown that logic circuits of size between 2000 to 5000 gates are best handled by a logic optimizer. This implies that in a Verilog HDL model, always statements must not be inordinately long. A design should be structured into multiple always statements or multiple modules.

There is no correlation between the gates produced and the number of lines of Verilog HDL code. A 2500-gate circuit could have been synthesized from a 10-line Verilog HDL code (may have a for-loop and/or vectors) or from 10,000 lines of Verilog HDL code (maybe from a large case statement with simple assignments).

Synthesis run-times, mainly logic optimization, are exponential with design size. Thus it is critical to keep the sizes of sub-blocks within a design manageable.

Hierarchy

It is useful to retain the hierarchy of a Verilog HDL model in terms of always statements. This enables a hierarchy of sub-circuits to be produced by the synthesis tool that a logic optimizer can effectively handle.

Quite often, a synthesis tool might automatically preserve the hierarchy of a large datapath operator. For example,

```
reg [15:0] Zim, Rim, Sim;
. . .
Zim = Rim + Sim;
. . .
```

In this case, a synthesis tool may preserve the 16-bit adder as a separate hierarchy.

Macros as Structure

Synthesis is not the right mechanism to build a memory such as a ROM or a RAM. RAMs are usually available predefined in a technology library. When a module such as a RAM is required, it is better to treat this as a component, instantiate this in the model, and then synthesize the instantiating model. A synthesis tool merely creates a black box for the RAM into which the designer would later link in the RAM module.

Similar actions may be necessary if a designer has a statement of the form:

```
Cyr = Rby * Ytr ;          // 16-bit arguments.
```

and expects the synthesis tool to implement an efficient multiplier. The designer may have a better designed multiplier. Again in this case, it is better for the designer to instantiate a multiplier as a component, rather than use a multiplication operator which, upon synthesis, may or may not produce an efficient multiplier.

4.9 Using Parentheses

When writing Verilog HDL code, the designer must be aware of the logic structure being generated. One such important point is the use of parentheses. Here is an example.

```
Result = Rhi + Rlo - PhyData + MacReset;
```

A synthesis tool when synthesizing the right-hand-side expression follows the Verilog HDL rules for expression evaluation, that is, left to right, and builds a circuit as shown in Figure 4-4. The logic structure generated may

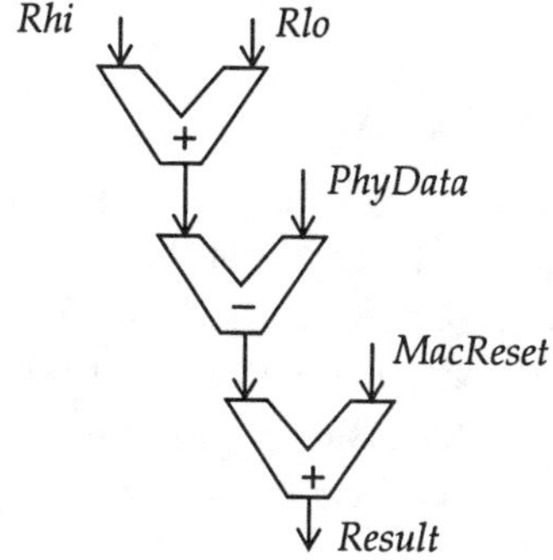

Figure 4-4 Without using parentheses.

end up having a longer critical path. A better alternative is to use parentheses, such as:

```
Result = (Rhi + Rlo) - (PhyData - MacReset);
```

which results in a smaller critical path. The synthesized circuit is shown in Figure 4-5. Using parentheses may also help identify opportunities for identifying common subexpressions.

Recommendation: Use parentheses liberally in an expression to control the structure of the synthesized logic.

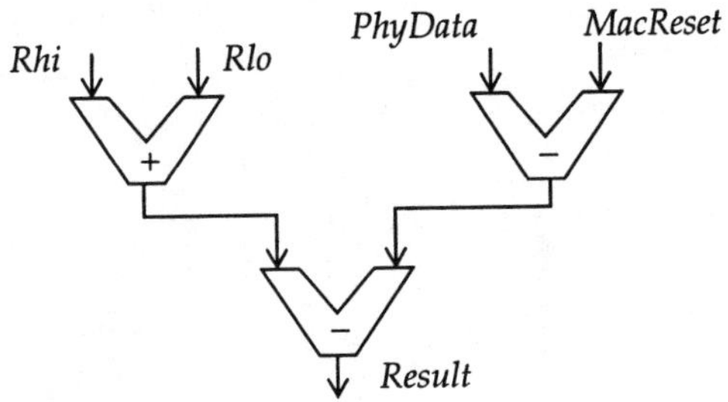

Figure 4-5 After using parentheses.

❑

CHAPTER

5

VERIFICATION

Having synthesized a Verilog HDL model into a netlist, it is important to verify the functionality of the synthesized netlist to ensure that it still matches the intended functionality. This step is important since a synthesis system may make certain assumptions or interpretations of the Verilog HDL code that may not match those intended by the model writer.

In this chapter, we assume that this verification step is performed using simulation which verifies the functionality between the design model and its synthesized netlist. We illustrate some cases of functional mismatches between the design model and its synthesized netlist that might possibly occur, describe their cause, and provide recommendations for avoiding them.

In this chapter, we assume that the synthesis process produces a synthesized netlist in Verilog HDL as shown in Figure 5-1. A Verilog HDL netlist is a collection of module instances interconnected by nets.

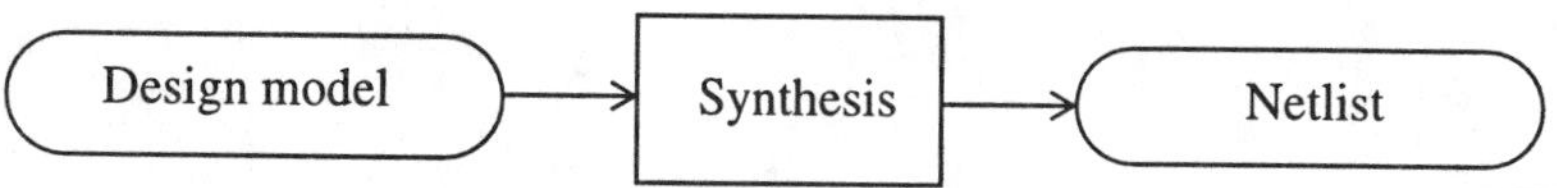

Figure 5-1 A netlist is produced from synthesis.

5.1 A Test Bench

One approach to verifying functionality is to simulate the netlist with the same set of stimulus as used during design model simulation, save the results in a results file and compare to see if the results are identical. This scenario is shown in Figure 5-2.

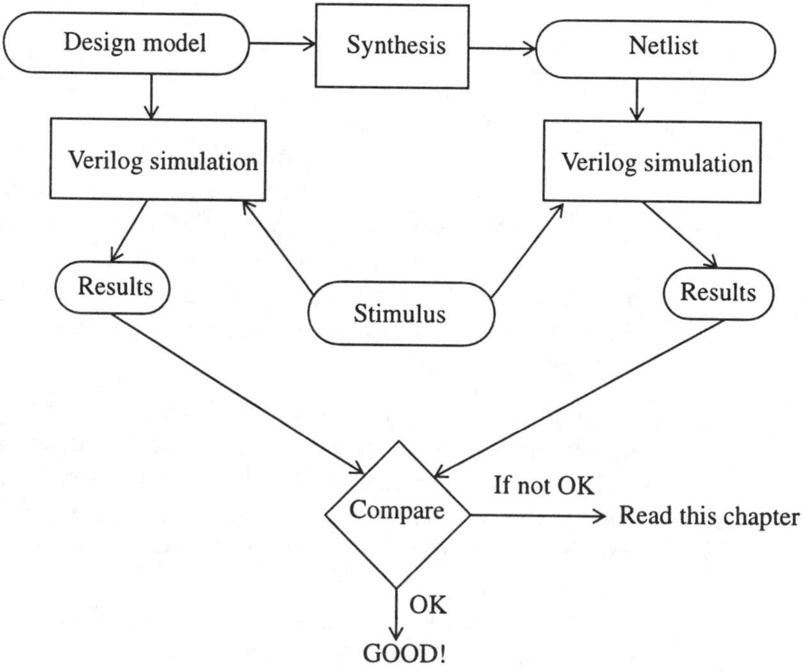

Figure 5-2 Verification by simulation.

Another approach is to write a test bench; a test bench is a model written in Verilog HDL that applies stimulus, compares the output responses, and reports any functional mismatches. Figure 5-3 shows such a scenario. A test bench for a full-adder is shown next. The stimulus is read from a vector file "Inputs.vec"; its contents are of the form:

```
100
000
101
011
111
```

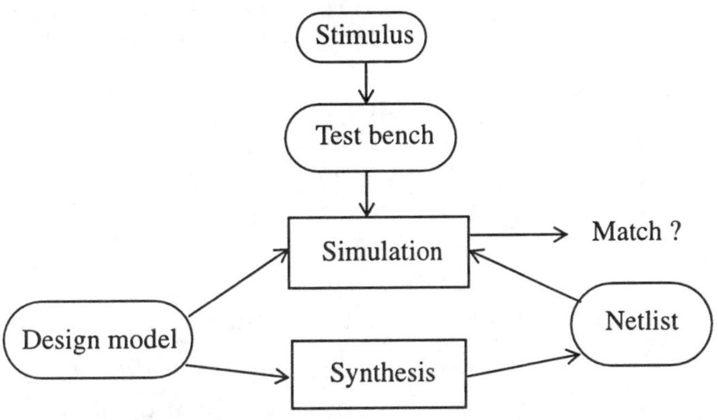

Figure 5-3 Using a common test bench.

```
module TestBenchFA;
  parameter WORDS = 5;
  reg [1:3] MemV [1:WORDS];
  reg A, B, Cin;
  wire SumBeh, CoutBeh, SumStr, CoutStr;
  integer J;

  // Instantiate the design module under test:
  FA_RTL F1 (A, B, Cin, SumBeh, CoutBeh);

  // Instantiate the synthesized netlist module:
  FA_Netlist F2 (A, B, Cin, SumStr, CoutStr);
```

```
    initial
      begin
        // Read the file with input vectors:
        $readmemb ("Inputs.vec", MemV);

        // Apply each vector to both design module and
        // synthesized netlist module:
        for (J = 1; J <= WORDS; J = J + 1)
        begin
          {A, B, Cin} = MemV[J];
          #5; // Wait for 5 time units for circuit to settle.

          // If output values do not match:
          if ((SumBeh !== SumStr) || (CoutBeh !== CoutStr))
            $display ("****Mismatch on vector %b *****",
                      MemV[J]);
          else
            $display ("No mismatch on vector %b", MemV[J]);
        end
    end
  endmodule
```

This test bench prints all mismatch violations that occur.

In the following sections, we see examples of how mismatches may occur that may be caused due to different interpretations by synthesis (as compared to Verilog HDL language semantics).

5.2 Delays in Assignment Statements

Delays specified in a design model may cause a functional mismatch between the model and the synthesized netlist. Here is an example of an adder model that uses a delay in a continuous assignment, and its synthesized netlist.

```
module Adder (A, B, C);
  input [0:3] A, B;
  output [0:3] C;

  assign #5 C = A + B;
endmodule
```

```
// The synthesized netlist is:
module AdderNetList (A0, A1, A2, A3, B0, B1, B2, B3,
                     C0, C1, C2, C3);
  input A0, A1, A2, A3, B0, B1, B2, B3;
  output C0, C1, C2, C3;

  OAI21  C0_1     (C2_1, S248, S310, C0);
  ND2    S310_1   (S248, C2_1, S310);
  XOR2   S248_1   (A0, B0, S248);
  AOI22  C2_2     (S241, S244, A1, B1, C2_1);
  OAI22  C1_1     (S295, S244, S299, S241, C1);
  INRB   S299_1   (S244, S299);
  OAI22  S244_1   (B1, S242, A1, S243, S244);
  INRB   S243_1   (B1, S243);
  INRB   S242_1   (A1, S242);
  INRB   S295_1   (S241, S295);
  OAI22  S241_1   (S291, S237, S238, S239, S241);
  INRB   S291_1   (S240, S291);
  OAI21  C2_1     (S237, S240, S334, C2);
  ND2    S334_1   (S237, S240, S334);
  OAI22  S240_1   (B2, S238, A2, S239, S240);
  INRB   S239_1   (B2, S239);
  INRB   S238_1   (A2, S238);
  ND2    S237_1   (A3, B3, S237);
  OAI22  C3_1     (B3, S235, A3, S236, C3);
  INRB   S236_1   (B3, S236);
  INRB   S235_1   (A3, S235);
endmodule
```

If vectors from a stimulus file were applied, say every 1 ns, and all the module instances in the netlist represent behavioral models with no delay, the results between the design model and the netlist will be skewed because of the difference in delays. The correct approach in such a case is:

i. Either to delete all delays from the design model,

ii. Or to apply the stimulus with a period greater than 5 ns: a better rule.

When delays are present in the models for the library modules, these delays must also be considered in determining the stimulus period.

Recommendation: To avoid delays in a design model from causing functional mismatches, the maximum delay in the model must be computed. The stimulus application time must be greater than this maximum delay.

5.3 Unconnected Ports

It could happen that a synthesized netlist has a module instance with an unconnected input port. Such a case is shown in the following example.

```
module AOI22 (A, B, D, Z);
  input A, B, D;
  output Z;
  reg T1, T2, C;

  always @ (A or B or D)
  begin
    T1 = A & B;
    T2 = C & D;          // C is never assigned a value.
    Z = ! (T1 | T2);
  end
endmodule

// Its synthesized netlist is:
module AOI22_NetList (A, B, D, Z);
  input A, B, D;
  output Z;

  AND2    S0_1    ( A, B, T1_1);
  AND2    S1_1    ( , D, T2_1);    // First port is open.
  OR2     S2_1    ( T1_1, T2_1, T2_0);
  INRB    S3_1    ( T2_0, Z);
endmodule
// Note: A logic optimizer has not yet been used; it
// could potentially remove a redundant gate.
```

Notice that in the synthesized netlist, the first input of the *AND2* module instance *S1_1* is open. During the simulation of module *AOI22_NetList*, the open input takes the value z[i], whereas the unassigned value of *C* in module *AOI22*[ii] takes on a default value of x. The fact that different values are used for *C* during the design model simulation and the synthesized netlist simulation, a potential exists for functional mismatch to occur due to different values being the default in the two different domains.

Recommendation: A good synthesis system will issue warning messages about a value used before being assigned (such as variable *C* in the module *AOI22*). Pay attention to these warnings.

5.4 Missing Latches

In Chapter 2, we described rules for inferring latches. We also described an exception to the rule, that is, a variable does not infer a latch if it is used as a temporary. However, there are a few other cases where a variable may not infer a latch, even though it appears from the code sequence that it should.

Let us consider the first case.

```
wire Control, Jrequest;
reg DebugX;
. . .
always @ (Control or Jrequest)
  if (Control)
    DebugX = Jrequest;
  else
    DebugX = DebugX;
```

In this always statement, variable *DebugX* is assigned in all branches of the `if` statement. However, data flow analysis reveals that the value of *DebugX* needs to be saved (since its value is used before an assignment when *Control* is false). In this case, a synthesis system may produce a warning message about variable *DebugX* being used before its assignment and also about a potential functional mismatch that may occur between the design model and its synthesized netlist.

Let us reiterate the rules for inferring latches once more:

---

i. In Verilog HDL, an unassigned variable of reg type has a default value of x and a variable of a net type has a default value of z.

ii. Behavior of logic gates used in the synthesized netlists are described in Appendix B.

i. A variable is assigned in a conditional statement (`if` or case), and

ii. Variable is NOT assigned in all branches of the conditional statement, and

iii. Value of variable needs to be saved between multiple invocations of the always statement.

All the three conditions must be satisfied before a variable is inferred as a latch. In the above always statement, *DebugX* violates rule (ii). Therefore no latch is produced for *DebugX*.

Here is another example.

```
always @ (Control)
begin
  if (Control)
    DebugX = Jrequest;
  else
    DebugX = Bdy;

  Bdy = DebugX;
end
```

In this always statement, it appears that there should be a latch for either *DebugX* or *Bdy*. There is no latch for *DebugX* since it violates rule (ii). There is no latch for *Bdy* since it violates rule (i). Language semantics however indicate that value for *Bdy* needs to be saved. A synthesis system in this case may not produce a latch; instead it may issue a warning message about *Bdy* being used before its assignment and in addition, produce a warning message about a potential for functional mismatch that may occur.

In the following always statement, no latch is produced for *DebugX* since it violates rule (ii) but a latch is produced for *Bdy*.

```
always @ (Control)
begin
  if (Control)
    DebugX = Jrequest;
  else
    DebugX = Bdy;
```

```
  if (Jrequest)
    Bdy = DebugX;
end
```

What about the following always statement?

```
always @ (Control)
begin
  if (Control)
    DebugX = Jrequest;
  else
    DebugX = Bdy;

  if (Jrequest)
    Bdy = DebugX;
  else
    Bdy = 'b1;
end
```

There are no latches for *DebugX* and *Bdy*. However language semantics indicate that *Bdy* needs to be saved. A synthesis system may not produce a latch; it may generate a warning about the variable being used before its assignment and that there is a potential for a functional mismatch.

5.5 More on Delays

Delays are often ignored by a synthesis system. The fact that they are ignored may simply cause simulation results to differ between the synthesized netlist and the design model. A case in point.

```
LX = #3 'b1;

if (CondA)
  LX = #5 'b0;
  . . .
```

Model simulation shows a value of 1 on *LX* after 3 ns and the value going to 0 after 5 ns if the condition *CondA* is true. However, since a synthesis system ignores delays, if *CondA* is true, the net effect is as if a 0 is assigned to *LX* and the appropriate hardware gets synthesized to reflect this. Notice that if the synthesized netlist is simulated, the value of *LX* will not go to 1 if *CondA* is true.

Recommendation: Avoid inserting delays into a design model that is to be synthesized. If necessary, lump total delays for a variable in one place.

5.6 Event List

Quite often, a synthesis system ignores the event list of an always statement during synthesis. This can lead to functional mismatches if proper care is not taken in modeling. Here is a simple example.

```
always @ (Read)
  Grt = Read & Clock;
// Synthesized netlist is shown in Figure 5-4.
```

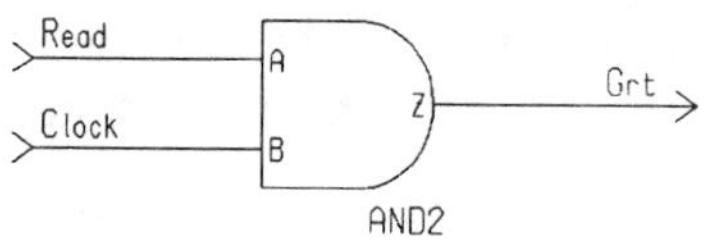

Figure 5-4 Netlist is sensitive to both *Read* and *Clock*.

The synthesized netlist, as shown in Figure 5-4, evaluates on all changes of *Read* and *Clock*, while the always statement executes only on changes to *Read*.

Here is another example of an always statement with an incomplete event list that may cause functional mismatches.

```
reg Rst;
reg [3:0] Pbus, Treg;
. . .
always @ (Rst)
  if (Rst)
    Treg = 0;
```

```
else
  Treg = Pbus;
```

The variable *Pbus* is not in the event list of the always statement. However in the synthesized netlist, any changes on *Pbus* will propagate into *Treg* if the `if` condition is false. This is not consistent with the design model semantics and thus a functional mismatch occurs.

Recommendation: For an always statement without a clock event (that is, when modeling combinational logic), include all variables read in the always statement in the event list.

5.7 Synthesis Directives

The two synthesis directives we have seen so far, full_case and parallel_case, can potentially cause functional mismatches to occur between the design model and the synthesized netlist. The problem is that these directives are recognized only by a synthesis tool and not by a simulation tool. In either of the cases, if the designer is not careful in specifying the directive, mismatches can occur.

Here is an example of a full_case synthesis directive.

```
reg [1:0] CurrentState, NextState;
. . .
case (CurrentState)              // synthesis full_case
  2'b01 : NextState = 2'b10;
  2'b10 : NextState = 2'b01;
endcase
```

The full_case directive tells the synthesis tool that all possible values that can possibly occur in *CurrentState* have been listed and the value of *NextState* is a don't-care for all other cases, and therefore, the synthesis tool should not generate latches for *NextState*. However this may not be true in simulation. It could happen that *CurrentState* for some reason, gets a value of 2'b00. In such a case, the case statement simulates as if *NextState* value is saved, but in the synthesized netlist, the value of *NextState* may not be saved.

Here is an example of a parallel_case synthesis directive.

```
case (1'b1)                // synthesis parallel_case
  Gate1 : Mask1 = 1;
  Gate2 : Mask2 = 1;
  Gate3 : Mask3 = 1;
endcase
```

Simulation semantics of the case statement (the parallel_case directive is ignored since it is a comment) specifies that if *Gate1* is a 1, then assign 1 to *Mask1*, else if *Gate2* is a 1, assign 1 to *Mask2*, else if *Gate3* is a 1, assign 1 to *Mask3*. However, with the parallel_case directive, instead of a priority if-structure being synthesized, a parallel decoder is synthesized. This can cause functional mismatches to occur. What if both *Gate3* and *Gate1* were 1 at the same time? In the case statement, the first branch is taken, whereas in the synthesized netlist, both branches 1 and 3 are enabled. Here is the semantics for the case statement expressed using an `if` statement.

```
if (Gate1)
  Mask1 = 1;
else if (Gate2)
  Mask2 = 1;
else if (Gate3)
  Mask3 = 1;
```

This is the semantics of the synthesized netlist.

```
if (Gate1)
  Mask1 = 1;

if (Gate2)
  Mask2 = 1;

if (Gate3)
  Mask3 = 1;
```

Recommendation: Use caution when using the synthesis directives: full_case and parallel_case. Use only if really necessary.

5.8 Variable Asynchronous Preset

When synthesizing an asynchronous preset clear flip-flop, the recommendation is to assign only constant values under the asynchronous conditions. If a variable is asynchronously read, there is a potential for a functional mismatch to occur. Here is an example.

```
module VarPreset (ClkZ, PreLoad, LoadData, PrintBus,
                  QuickBus);
  input ClkZ, PreLoad;
  input [1:0] LoadData, PrintBus;
  output [1:0] QuickBus;
  reg [1:0] QuickBus;

  always @(negedge PreLoad or posedge ClkZ)
    if (! PreLoad)
      QuickBus <= LoadData; // Asynchronous data assign.
    else
      QuickBus <= PrintBus;
endmodule
// Synthesized netlist is shown in Figure 5-5.
```

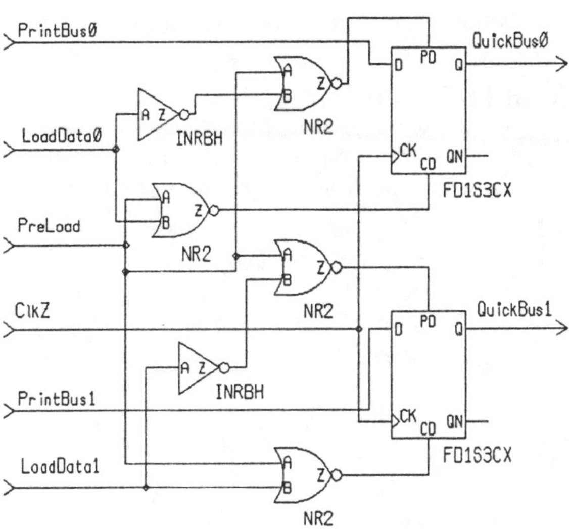

Figure 5-5 Variable asynchronous preset.

Two flip-flops with asynchronous preset and clear are synthesized for the variable *QuickBus*. The variable *LoadData* is connected to the preset clear inputs of the flip-flops through other logic. When *PreLoad* is active (is 0) and *LoadData* changes, the outputs of the flip-flops are immediately affected because of the asynchronous data change. However in the design model, any change on *LoadData* has no effect on the output *QuickBus*. Thus there is a mismatch.

Recommendation: Avoid asynchronously reading a variable and assigning it to a flip-flop; else ensure that there are no changes on asynchronous data when the asynchronous conditions are active.

5.9 Blocking and Non-blocking Assignments

In Chapter 2, we recommended that:

- blocking assignments be used for modeling combinational logic, and
- non-blocking assignments be used for modeling sequential logic; blocking assignments may be used for variables that are assigned and used, all within an always statement.

In this section, we explain why this recommendation is important to be followed; else there is a risk of getting functional mismatches.

5.9.1 Combinational Logic

Blocking assignments mirror the dataflow in a combinational circuit. Consider the following always statement.

```
reg TM, TN, TO, TZ;

always @ (A or B or C or D or E)
begin
  TM = A & B;
  TN = C & D;
  TO = TM | TN | E;
  TZ = ! TO;
end
```

All the assignments are blocking assignments. Statements within the sequential block imply to compute the value of *TM* first, then execute the second statement, assign to *TN*, then go to third statement, assign to *TO*, and so on. This mimics the dataflow through the combinational logic.

Let us now change all these to non-blocking assignments.

```
reg TM, TN, TO, TZ;

always @ (A or B or C or D or E)
begin
  TM <= A & B;
  TN <= C & D;
  TO <= TM | TN | E;
  TZ <= ! TO;
end
```

When the first assignment statement executes, *TM* does not get updated immediately but is scheduled to be assigned at the end of the current simulation cycle. Since all statement executions occur sequentially and in zero time, so when the third statement is executed, the old value of *TM* is used to compute the value of *TO* (*TM* has not been assigned its new value yet). Consequently, the output *TZ* does not reflect the and-or-invert behavior of the logic. The problem is that *TM*, *TN*, and *TO* all get updated at the end of the current simulation cycle and these updated values are not used again to reevaluate the logic.

A solution to this problem is to place variables *TM*, *TN* and *TO* also in the event list of the always statement, such as:

```
reg TM, TN, TO, TZ;

always @ (A or B or C or D or E or TM or TN or TO)
begin
  TM <= A & B;
  TN <= C & D;
  TO <= TM | TN | E;
  TZ <= ! TO;
end
```

In this case, when *TM*, *TN* or *TO* changes, the always statement is re-evaluated and eventually *TZ* does get the correct value. So there are two problems that have been identified:

- non-blocking assignments do not show the logical flow
- need to put all targets of assignments in the event list

These problems can simply be avoided by using blocking assignments when modeling combinational logic and are therefore recommended.

5.9.2 Sequential Logic

Let us first consider what happens if blocking assignments are exclusively used for modeling sequential logic. Consider the following two always statements.

```
always @(posedge ClkA)          // Label AwA
  . . . = DataOut;              // Read value of DataOut.

always @(posedge ClkA)          // Label AwB
  DataOut = . . .;              // Using blocking assignment.
```

The always statement, labeled *AwB*, assigns a value to *DataOut* in a blocking fashion and the always statement, labeled *AwA*, reads the value of *DataOut*. If these always statements were simulated in the sequence shown (a simulator orders the always statements to be executed in sequence based on event changes in the event list), and if *ClkA* had a positive edge, the always statement *AwA* reads the current value of *DataOut* first and then the always statement *AwB* causes a new value to be assigned to *DataOut*. If the order of the always statements were reversed (or if a simulator chooses to reorder the execution of the always statements), execution of the always statement *AwB* occurs first causing *DataOut* to be assigned a new value in zero time. Subsequently, the read of *DataOut* in the always statement *AwA* uses the new updated value of *DataOut*. Thus it appears that depending on the order in which the always statements are executed, different results are obtained. The problem is really caused by the fact that when both always statements are ready for execution, the assignment to *DataOut* occurs in zero time and completes. So depending on which always statements gets executed first, the read of *DataOut* in *AwA* will either be an old value of *DataOut* or a new value of *DataOut*.

To avoid this simulation behavior dependence, it is best to force the assignment to occur at a later time, a time after which all reads are guaranteed to have been completed. This can be achieved by using the non-blocking assignment. In such a case, the read of *DataOut* occurs at the current time, while a new value is assigned to *DataOut* at the end of the current simulation step (that is, after all reads are completed). This makes the behavior of the model insensitive to the order of the always statements. Here are the always statements with non-blocking assignments used.

```
always @(posedge ClkA)      // Label AwA
  . . . = DataOut;          // Read value of DataOut.

always @(posedge ClkA)      // Label AwB
  DataOut <= . . .;       // Using non-blocking assignment.
```

So we see that if a variable is assigned a value in one always statement and its value read external to that always statement, the assignment should be a non-blocking procedural assignment.

What if the assignment and reading of a variable all occur in the same clocked always statement? In such a case, blocking assignments may be used.

```
reg [9:0] Total;

always @(negedge ClkB)
begin
  Total = LoadValue + 2;        // Blocking assignment.

  if (Total == 21)       // Value assigned in previous
                         // statement used.
    NumBus <= ControlBus;
  else
    NumBus <= DataBus;
end
```

Total is a variable assigned and then read within the same always statement. In this case, we would like the assignment to *Total* to be completed before the `if` condition is evaluated. *Total* is a temporary; a value is assigned to it and then read. Thus a blocking assignment is suitable for *Total*.

If a non-blocking assignment is used, such as:

```
reg [9:0] Total;

always @(negedge ClkB)
begin
  Total <= LoadValue + 2;      // Non-blocking assignment.

  if (Total == 21)             // Old value of Total read.
    NumBus <= ControlBus;
  else
    NumBus <= DataBus;
end
```

then the value of *Total* when the `if` condition is evaluated is the old value of *Total*, not the value that is scheduled to be assigned to it in the previous assignment.

Therefore, the recommendation is to use non-blocking assignments for variables that are read outside of the always statement in which they are assigned. Additionally, for variables that are assigned and used only within an always statement, use blocking assignments.

❑

APPENDIX

SYNTHESIZABLE CONSTRUCTS

To give an idea of what Verilog HDL constructs are synthesizable, this appendix provides a listing of the synthesizable Verilog HDL constructs that are recognized by the ArchSyn synthesis system, v14.0. This subset may not be the same for all synthesis tools.

Constructs that have relevance only to simulation, and not to synthesis, are identified as "ignored constructs" and constructs that are not synthesizable are marked as "not supported". The constructs are categorized as follows:

i. *Supported*: Constructs that get synthesized into hardware.

ii. *Not supported*: Synthesis terminates when such a construct is present in the input file.

iii. *Ignored*: Warning messages are issued during synthesis, except for declarations.

In the following tables, the first column specifies the Verilog HDL feature, the second column indicates whether the feature is supported or not, and the third column is for comments and exceptions.

Lexical Conventions		
Operators	Supported	Case equality and case inequality not supported.
White Space and Comments	Supported	
Numbers	Supported	
Strings	Not supported	
Identifiers, Keywords, and System Names	Supported	System names are ignored.
Text Substitutions	Supported	

Data Types		
Value Set	Supported	
Registers and Nets	Supported	
Vectors	Supported	
Strengths	Ignored	
Implicit Declarations	Supported	
Net Initialization	Not supported	The wires are initially unconnected.
Net Types	Supported	
Memories	Supported	
Integers	Supported	
Times	Not supported	
Real Numbers	Not supported	
Parameters	Supported	

Expressions		
Operators	Supported	Case equality and case inequality not supported.
Operands		
Net and Register Bit Addressing	Supported	
Memory Addressing	Supported	
Strings	Not supported	
Minimum, Typical, Maximum Delay Expressions	Ignored	
Expression Bit Lengths	Supported	

Assignments		
Continuous Assignments	Supported	Delay values and drive strength values ignored.
Procedural Assignments	Supported	

Gate and Switch Level Modeling		
Gate and Switch Declaration Syntax	Supported	Strengths and delays not supported.
AND, NAND, NOR, OR, XOR, and XNOR Gates	Supported	
BUF Gate	Supported	
NOT Gate	Supported	
BUFIF1, BUFIF0, NOTIF1, and NOTIF0 Gates	Supported	
MOS Switches	Not supported	

Gate and Switch Level Modeling		
Bidirectional Pass Switches	Not supported	
CMOS Gates	Not supported	
PULLUP and PULL-DOWN Sources	Not supported	
Implicit Net Declarations	Supported	
Logic Strength Modeling	Not supported	
Strengths and Values of Combined Signals	Not supported	
Mnemonic Format	Not supported	
Strength Reduction by Non-Resistive Devices	Not supported	
Strength Reduction by Resistive Devices	Not supported	
Strengths of Net Types	Ignored	
Gate and Net Delays	Ignored	
Gate and Net Name Removal	Not supported	

User-Defined Primitives		
	Not Supported	

Behavioral Modeling		
Procedural Assignments	Supported	Time declaration is not supported. Timing controls as delays are ignored. Timing controls as events are not supported.

Behavioral Modeling		
Conditional Statement	Supported	
Case Statement	Supported	
Looping Statements		
Forever Loop	Not supported	
Repeat Loop	Supported	Repeat expression has to be a constant.
While Loop	Not supported	
For Loop	Supported	Assignments to the FOR index have to be constant assignments.
Procedural Timing Controls		Delay timing controls are ignored, event timing controls are not supported.
Block Statements	Supported	Time declaration, and event declaration are not supported.
Structured Procedure		
Initial Statement	Ignored	
Always Statement	Supported	
Task	Supported	Time and event declarations are not supported.
Function	Supported	Time declaration, and event declaration are not supported.

Tasks and Functions		
Tasks and Task Enabling	Supported	Time and event declarations are not supported.
Functions and Function Calling	Supported	Time declaration and event declaration are not supported

Disabling of Named Blocks and Tasks		
	Not supported	

Procedural Continuous Assignments		
	Not supported	

Hierarchical Structures		
Modules	Supported	
Top-Level Modules	Supported	
Module Instantiation	Supported	
Overriding Module Parameter Values	Supported	DEFPARAM is not supported.
Macro Modules	Supported	
Ports	Supported	
Hierarchical Names	Not supported	
Automatic Naming	Supported	System generated names not supported.
Scope Rules	Supported	

Specify Blocks		
	Not supported	

❑

APPENDIX

B

A GENERIC LIBRARY

This appendix describes the components used in the synthesized netlists shown in the text. Functionality of each component is specified using comments.

```
module AND2 (A, B, Z);
  input A, B;
  output Z;
  // Z = A & B;
endmodule

module AOI21 (A1, A2, B, Z);
  input A1, A2, B;
  output Z;
  // Z = ! ((A1 & A2) | B);
endmodule
```

```
module AOI211 (A1, A2, B1, B2, Z);
  input A1, A2, B1, B2;
  output Z;
  // Z = ! ((A1 & A2) | B1 | B2);
endmodule

module AOI22 (A1, A2, B1, B2, Z);
  input A1, A2, B1, B2;
  output Z;
  // Z = ! ((A1 & A2) | (B1 & B2));
endmodule

module BN20T20D (A, ST, STN, PADI, Z, PADO);
  input A, ST, STN, PADI;
  output Z, PADO;
  // Bidirectional buffer.
  // Z = PADI;
  // PADO =  0 when (!A && !STN) else
  //         1 when (A && ST) else
  //         'bz;
endmodule

module BUF (A, Z);
  input A;
  output Z;
  // Z = A;
endmodule

module FD1P3AX (D, SP, CK, Q, QN);
  input D, SP, CK;
  output Q, QN;
  // Positive edge-triggered, positive-level sample,
  // static D-type FF.
endmodule

module FD1S1A (D, CK, Q, QN);
  input D, CK;
  output Q, QN;
  // Positive-level sense static D-type FF (latch).
endmodule
```

```
module FD1S1B (D, CK, PD, Q, QN);
  input D, CK, PD;
  output Q, QN;
  // Positive-level sense, positive asynchronous
  // preset, static D-type FF (latch).
endmodule

module FD1S1D (D, CK, CD, Q, QN);
  input D, CK, CD;
  output Q, QN;
  // Positive-level sense, positive asynchronous
  // clear, static D-type FF (latch).
endmodule

module FD1S1E (D, CK, CDN, Q, QN);
  input D, CK, CDN;
  output Q, QN;
  // Positive-level sense, negative asynchronous clear,
  // static D-type FF (latch).
endmodule

module FD1S1F (D, CK, PD, CDN, Q, QN);
  input D, CK, PD, CDN;
  output Q, QN;
  // Positive-level sense, negative asynchronous clear,
  // positive asynchronous preset, static
  // D-type FF (latch).
endmodule

module FD1S2AX (D, CK, Q, QN);
  input D, CK;
  output Q, QN;
  // Negative edge-triggered, static D-type FF.
endmodule

module FD1S2BX (D, CK, PD, Q, QN);
  input D, CK, PD;
  output Q, QN;
  // Negative edge-triggered, positive asynchronous
  // preset, static D-type FF.
endmodule
```

```
module FD1S2CX (D, CK, PD, Q, QN);
  input D, CK, PD;
  output Q, QN;
  // Negative edge-triggered, positive asynchronous
  // preset, positive asynchronous clear,
  // static D-type FF.
endmodule

module FD1S2DX (D, CK, CD, Q, QN);
  input D, CK, CD;
  output Q, QN;
  // Negative edge-triggered, positive asynchronous
  // clear, static D-type FF.
endmodule

module FD1S2EX (D, CK, CDN, Q, QN);
  input D, CK, CDN;
  output Q, QN;
  // Negative edge-triggered, negative asynchronous
  // clear, static D-type FF.
endmodule

module FD1S2FX (D, CK, PD, CDN, Q, QN);
  input D, CK, PD, CDN;
  output Q, QN;
  // Negative edge-triggered, negative asynchronous
  // clear, positive asynchronous preset, static
  // D-type FF.
endmodule

module FD1S2GX (D, CK, PD, CDN, Q, QN);
  input D, CK, PD, CDN;
  output Q, QN;
  // Negative edge-triggered, negative asynchronous
  // preset, static D-type FF.
endmodule

module FD1S2IX (D, CK, CD, Q, QN);
  input D, CK, CD;
  output Q, QN;
  // Negative edge-triggered, positive synchronous
```

```
  // clear, static D-type FF.
endmodule

module FD1S2JX (D, CK, PD, Q, QN);
  input D, CK, PD;
  output Q, QN;
  // Negative edge-triggered, positive synchronous
  // preset, static D-type FF.
endmodule

module FD1S2NX (D, CK, PDN, CD, Q, QN);
  input D, CK, PDN, CD;
  output Q, QN;
  // Negative edge-triggered, positive asynchronous
  // clear, negative asynchronous preset, static
  // D-type FF.
endmodule

module FD1S2OX (D, CK, PD, CD, Q, QN);
  input D, CK, PD, CD;
  output Q, QN;
  // Negative edge-triggered, positive synchronous
  // clear, positive synchronous preset, static
  // D-type FF.
endmodule

module FD1S3AX (D, CK, Q, QN);
  input D, CK;
  output Q, QN;
  // Positive edge-triggered, static D-type FF.
endmodule

module FD1S3BX (D, CK, Q, QN);
  input D, CK;
  output Q, QN;
  // Positive edge-triggered, positive asynchronous
  // preset, static D-type FF.
endmodule

module FD1S3CX (D, CK, Q, QN);
  input D, CK;
  output Q, QN;
```

```
  // Positive edge-triggered, positive asynchronous
  // clear, positive asynchronous preset, static
  // D-type FF.
endmodule

module FD1S3EX (D, CK, CDN, Q, QN);
  input D, CK, CDN;
  output Q, QN;
  // Positive edge-triggered, negative synchronous
  // clear, static D-type FF.
endmodule

module FL1S2AX (D0, D1, CK, SD, Q, QN);
  input D0, D1, CK, SD;
  output Q, QN;
  // Negative edge-triggered, data select front end,
  // scan FF.
endmodule

module FL1S2EX (D0, D1, CK, SD, CDN, Q, QN);
  input D0, D1, CK, SD, CDN;
  output Q, QN;
  // Negative edge-triggered, data select front end,
  // negative asynchronous clear, scan FF.
endmodule

module FL1S3AX (D0, D1, CK, SD, Q, QN);
  input D0, D1, CK, SD;
  output Q, QN;
  // Positive edge-triggered, data select front end,
  // scan FF.
endmodule

module FL1S3CX (D0, D1, CK, SD, Q, QN);
  input D0, D1, CK, SD;
  output Q, QN;
  // Positive edge-triggered, data select front end,
  // positive asynchronous clear, positive asynchronous
  // preset, scan FF.
  endmodule
```

```
module FL1S3EX (D0, D1, CK, SD, CDN, Q, QN);
  input D0, D1, CK, SD, CDN;
  output Q, QN;
  // Positive edge-triggered, data select front end,
  // negative asynchronous clear, scan FF.
endmodule

module FS0S1D (S, R, CD, Q, QN);
  input S, R, CD;
  output Q, QN;
  // Positive-level S input, positive-level R input,
  // positive asynchronous clear, R-S FF (latch).
endmodule

module INRB (A, Z);
  input A;
  output Z;
  // Z = ! A;
endmodule

module INRBH (A, Z);
  input A;
  output Z;
  // Z = ! A; (same as INRB)
endmodule

module ND2 (A, B, Z);
  input A, B;
  output Z;
  // Z = ! (A & B);
endmodule

module ND3 (A, B, C, Z);
  input A, B, C;
  output Z;
  // Z = ! (A & B & C);
endmodule

module ND4 (A, B, C, D, Z);
  input A, B, C, D;
  output Z;
```

```
  // Z = ! (A & B & C & D);
endmodule

module NR2 (A, B, Z);
  input A, B;
  output Z;
  // Z = ! (A | B);
endmodule

module NR3 (A, B, C, Z);
  input A, B, C;
  output Z;
  // Z = ! (A | B | C);
endmodule

module NR4 (A, B, C, D, Z);
  input A, B, C, D;
  output Z;
  // Z = ! (A | B | C | D);
endmodule

module OAI21 (A1, A2, B, Z);
  input A1, A2, B;
  output Z;
  // Z = ! ((A1 | A2) & B);
endmodule

module OAI22 (A1, A2, B1, B2, Z);
  input A1, A2, B1, B2;
  output Z;
  // Z = ! ((A1| A2) & (B1 | B2));
endmodule

module OAI4321 (A1, A2, A3, A4, B1, B2, B3, C1, C2, D, Z);
  input A1, A2, A3, A4, B1, B2, B3, C1, C2, D;
  output Z;
  // Z = ! ((A1 | A2 | A3 | A4) & (B1 | B2 | B3)
  //      & (C1 & C2) & D);
endmodule
```

```
module OR2 (A, B, Z);
  input A, B;
  output Z;
  // Z = A | B;
endmodule

module OR4 (A, B, C, D, Z);
  input A, B, C, D;
  output Z;
  // Z = A | B | C | D;
endmodule

module TBUS (D, CK, CKN, Q);
  input D, CK, CKN;
  output Q;
  // Q =  'bz when (! CK && CKN),
  //      'b0 when (CK && ! D),
  //      'b1 when (! CKN && D);
endmodule

module XNOR2 (A, B, Z);
  input A, B;
  output Z;
  // Z = | (A ^ B);
endmodule

module XOR2 (A, B, Z);
  input A, B;
  output Z;
  // Z = A ^ B;
endmodule

module XOR2Z (A, B, Z, Z1);
  input A, B;
  output Z, Z1;
  // Z = A ^ B; Z1 = ! (A | B);
endmodule
```

❑

BIBLIOGRAPHY

1. Bhasker J., *A Verilog HDL Primer*, Star Galaxy Press, Allentown, PA, 1997, ISBN 0-9656277-4-8.
2. *IEEE Standard Hardware Description Language Based on the Verilog Hardware Description Language*, IEEE Std 1364-1995, IEEE, 1995.
3. Lee James, *Verilog Quickstart*, Kluwer Academic, MA 1997, ISBN 0-7923992-7-7.
4. Palnitkar S., *Verilog HDL: A Guide to Digital Design and Synthesis*, Prentice Hall, NJ, 1996, ISBN 0-13-451675-3.
5. Sagdeo Vivek, *The Complete Verilog Book*, Kluwer Academic, MA, 1998, ISBN 0-7923818-8-2.
6. Smith Douglas, *HDL Chip Design*, Doone Publications, AL, 1996, ISBN 0-9651934-3-8.
7. Sternheim E., R. Singh and Y. Trivedi, *Digital Design with Verilog HDL*, Automata Publishing Company, CA, 1990, ISBN 0-9627488-0-3.
8. Thomas D. and P. Moorby, *The Verilog Hardware Description Language*, Kluwer Academic, MA, 1991, ISBN 0-7923912-6-8.

❑

INDEX

❑

Order Form

☆ **Fax orders**: (610) 391-7296

☆ **Telephone orders**: Call toll free (888) 727-7296

☆ **On-line orders**: SGalaxyPub@aol.com

☆ **Web site orders**: http://users.aol.com/SGalaxyPub

☆ **Postal orders**: Star Galaxy Publishing, Suite 401, 1058 Treeline Drive, Allentown, PA 18103.

Yes!!!! Please send me:

__ copies of *A VHDL Synthesis Primer, Second Edition* by J. Bhasker, ISBN 0-9650391-9-6, $59.95*

__ copies of *A Verilog HDL Primer* by J. Bhasker, ISBN 0-9656277-4-8, $59.95*

__ copies of *Verilog HDL Synthesis, A Practical Primer* by J. Bhasker, ISBN 0-9650391-5-3, $59.95*
* For orders of 3 or more, see http://users.aol.com/SGalaxyPub for discount schedule

I understand that I may return the books for a full refund - for any reason, no questions asked.

Name: ____

Address: ____

City: _________________________ State: _____ Zip: _________-_____

Telephone: (____) ________________ Email: ____________________

Sales tax:
Please add 6% for books shipped to Pennsylvania addresses.

Shipping:
❍ Delivery less than 1 week : $5.00 for first book, $0.50 for each additional book via UPS Ground or equivalent.
❍ Delivery 1 to 2 weeks : $3.00 per book via USPS Priority Mail
❍ International addresses: $7.00 to $15.00 per book via air mail depending on country

Payment:
❒ Cheque (payable to *Star Galaxy Publishing*)
❒ Credit card: ❍ VISA ❍ MasterCard ❍ AMEX
  ❒ Card number: ______________________________________
  ❒ Name on card:_________________________________Exp. date: _____/_____
  ❒ Signature: ____

Call *toll free* and order now!

Order Form

☆ **Fax orders**: (610) 391-7296

☆ **Telephone orders**: Call toll free (888) 727-7296

☆ **On-line orders**: SGalaxyPub@aol.com

☆ **Web site orders**: http://users.aol.com/SGalaxyPub

☆ **Postal orders**: Star Galaxy Publishing, Suite 401, 1058 Treeline Drive, Allentown, PA 18103.

Yes!!!! Please send me:

__ copies of *A VHDL Synthesis Primer, Second Edition* by J. Bhasker, ISBN 0-9650391-9-6, $59.95*

__ copies of *A Verilog HDL Primer* by J. Bhasker, ISBN 0-9656277-4-8, $59.95*

__ copies of *Verilog HDL Synthesis, A Practical Primer* by J. Bhasker, ISBN 0-9650391-5-3, $59.95*
* For orders of 3 or more, see http://users.aol.com/SGalaxyPub for discount schedule

I understand that I may return the books for a full refund - for any reason, no questions asked.

Name: ____

Address: ____

City: ______________________ State: ______ Zip: __________-_____

Telephone: (____) __________________ Email: ______________________

Sales tax:
Please add 6% for books shipped to Pennsylvania addresses.

Shipping:
❍ Delivery less than 1 week : $5.00 for first book, $0.50 for each additional book via UPS Ground or equivalent.
❍ Delivery 1 to 2 weeks : $3.00 per book via USPS Priority Mail
❍ International addresses: $7.00 to $15.00 per book via air mail depending on country

Payment:
❒ Cheque (payable to *Star Galaxy Publishing*)
❒ Credit card: ❍ VISA ❍ MasterCard ❍ AMEX
❒ Card number: ______________________________________
❒ Name on card:________________________________Exp. date: ______/______
❒ Signature: ______________________________________

Call *toll free* and order now!

林
紹
義
Shawyee Lin
9/12/2005
購
自
Amazon.com
$69.95